Course 2

Steck-Vaughn

REV it up!

Robust Encounters with Vocabulary

Isabel L. Beck, Ph.D., and
Margaret G. McKeown, Ph.D.

Steck Vaughn™

HOUGHTON MIFFLIN HARCOURT
Supplemental Publishers

www.SteckVaughn.com
800-531-5015

Acknowledgments

Literature

Grateful acknowledgment is given to the following publishers and copyright owners for permissions granted to reprint selections from their publications. All possible care has been taken to trace ownership and secure permission for each selection included. In the case of any errors or omissions, the Publisher will be pleased to make suitable acknowledgments in future editions.

p. 21, "The Struggle to Be an All-American Girl" by Elizabeth Wong.

p. 33, "My Father Is a Simple Man" is reprinted with permission from the publisher of *Sadness of Days* by Luis Omar Salinas (Arte Público Press—University of Houston, 1987)

p. 35, "I Remember My Father's Hands" by Lisa Suhair Majaj, reprinted by permission of the author

p. 57, Abridged from BETWEEN A ROCK AND A HARD PLACE by Aron Ralston. Copyright © 2004 by Aron Ralston. Reprinted with the permission of Atria Books, an imprint of Simon & Schuster Adult Publishing Group.

p. 70, From SOJOURNER TRUTH: AIN'T I A WOMAN? By Patricia and Frederick McKissack. Copyright © 1992 by Patricia C. McKissack. Reprinted by permission of Scholastic Inc.

p. 81, "Darkness at Noon" by Harold Krents from *The New York Times,* May 5, 1978. Copyright © 1978 by The New York Times Company. Reproduced by permission of the publisher.

p. 93, Excerpt from *The Time Traveler's Wife* by Audrey Niffenegger. Copyright © 1992 by Audrey Niffenegger. Reprinted by permission of MacAdam/Cage Publishing.

p. 106, "Neat People vs. Sloppy People" by Suzanne Britt, reprinted by permission of the author.

p. 118, "A Poem for Magic" by Quincy Troupe, reprinted by permission of the author.

p. 129, From THE STORY OF A SHIP-WRECKED SAILOR by Gabriel García Márquez, translated by Randolph Hogan, copyright © 1986 by Alfred A. Knopf Inc. Used by permission of Alfred A. Knopf, a division of Random House, Inc.

p. 141, From WHEN I WAS PUERTO RICAN by Esmeralda Santiago. Reprinted by permission of Da Capo Press, a member of Perseus Books Group.

p. 143, "Soul Food" by Janice Mirikitani. Reprinted by permission of the author.

p. 154, "What Is Intelligence, Anyway?" by Isaac Asimov. Published by permission of The Estate of Isaac Asimov c/o Ralph M. Vicinanza, Ltd.

p. 165, From FACING MOUNT KENYA by Jomo Kenyatta. Published 1962 by Vintage Books, an imprint of The Knopf Group, a division of Random House, Inc.

p. 178, "The Ordinary Son" from AT THE JIM BRIDGER, by Ron Carlson. Copyright © 2000 by Ron Carlson. Originally published in Esquire Magazine. Reprinted by permission of St. Martin's Press, LLC and Brandt and Hochman Literary Agents, Inc.

Cover photo ©Eduardo Garcia/Taxi/Getty Images.

Acknowledgments for photography and illustrations can be found on page 208.

Contents

1 **Short Story** ———————————————————————————— **8**

Surviving the Tryout
By Kelly Chausovsky

VOCABULARY

simultaneously	capsize
pervade	vague
merciless	trudge
mutiny	ravage
grotesque	stalwart

2 **Memoir** —————————————————————————————— **20**

The Struggle to Be an All-American Girl
By Elizabeth Wong

VOCABULARY

stoic	refinement
repress	pedestrian
maniacal	infuriate
painstakingly	condescending
lilting	contrite

3 **Poems** —————————————————————————————— **32**

My Father Is a Simple Man & I Remember My Father's Hands
By Luis Omar Salinas & Lisa Suhair Majaj

VOCABULARY

pretense	reminisce
fanfare	adulation
muted	laudable
secular	emulate
callous	exemplify

4 **Korean Folktale** _____ 44

The Tiger's Whisker
Retold by An Wei Chi

VOCABULARY

venerable	ponder
hermit	surreptitious
renowned	accustomed
indifferent	cantankerous
essential	placate

5 **Personal Narrative** _____ 56

Trapped
By Aron Ralston

VOCABULARY

pessimism	epiphany
rudimentary	reverberate
repulse	euphoric
vigorously	agonize
exasperate	methodical

6 **Biography** _____ 69

from Sojourner Truth: Ain't I a Woman?
By Patricia and Fredrick McKissack

VOCABULARY

congenial	deliberate
oppress	hypocrisy
subservient	chastise
discredit	advocate
hostile	galvanize

7 **Autobiographical Essay** ——————————————————— 80

Darkness at Noon
By Harold Krents

VOCABULARY

narcissistic	disposition
enunciate	exclusion
invariably	distinct
graphically	adversity
intone	bristle

8 **Novel Excerpt** ——————————————————— 92

Meeting Myself in a Museum
By Audrey Niffenegger

VOCABULARY

wary	recollect
wiry	omniscient
quizzical	emit
simulate	engross
equivocate	impressionable

9 **Essay** ——————————————————— 105

Neat People vs. Sloppy People
By Suzanne Britt

VOCABULARY

rectitude	sentimental
tentative	salvage
memento	swath
meticulous	haphazard
cavalier	satirical

10 **Poem** _____ 117

A Poem for "Magic"
By Quincy Troupe

VOCABULARY

wile	fervor
fusion	invigorating
deftly	lithe
frenzy	reverence
urgent	unequivocal

11 **Short Story Excerpt** _____ 128

from Fighting Off the Sharks for a Fish
By Gabriel García Márquez

VOCABULARY

agility	repugnant
disconcerting	palatable
voracious	appease
devour	dogged
protrude	livid

12 **Autobiographical Essay & Poem** _____ 140

How to Eat a Guava & Soul Food
By Esmeralda Santiago & Janice Mirikitani

VOCABULARY

embed	insinuate
tinge	autonomy
edible	unsurpassed
purse	affinity
exotic	evoke

13 **Essay** _____ 153

What Is Intelligence, Anyway?
By Isaac Asimov

VOCABULARY

aptitude	arbiter
complacent	indulgent
pronouncement	raucous
intricate	dupe
foist	divergent

14 **African Fable** _____ 164

The Jungle Commission
By Jomo Kenyatta

VOCABULARY

turmoil	relevant
impartiality	accommodate
authoritative	embroil
conclusive	annex
confine	disgruntled

15 **Short Story Excerpt** _____ 177

from The Ordinary Son
By Ron Carlson

VOCABULARY

fundamental	sanctum
prolong	condone
unkempt	idiosyncrasy
foster	innate
deprive	paradigm

16 **Short Story** _____ 189

based on The Open Window
By Saki

VOCABULARY

endeavor	infirmity
falter	discount
briskly	imminent
scarcity	devious
delusion	traumatized

Glossary _____ 201

Acknowledgments _____ 208

Surviving the TRYOUT

By Kelly Chausovsky
Illustrated by Ron Mahoney

Mari is determined to join her school's football team even though everyone tells her that girls don't play football. She knows she's talented, but can she make it through the tough, painful tryout?

Mari arranged the ball, the defenders and the goal into one line of sight and took a deep breath. She felt herself move forward, her steps lengthen, her right foot plant, and her left foot swing through the air and connect with the ball. She saw it soar up into a long, graceful arc, the white and black rotating clearly against the blue sky. She saw the line of yellow-and-gold uniforms jump simultaneously, straining for the ball, but it curved viciously over their heads and into the top corner of the goal. Her teammates' yells and cheers pervaded the field. Her overtime penalty kick had won the game!

Mari looked into the stands and saw Mr. Jackson, the football coach, smiling and writing something down on his clipboard. He looked up, caught her eye, and nodded.

Even though Mari Estella had grown up playing soccer, she had become more and more interested in American football as she got older. She liked the game itself, but there was something else that drove her. She had been told she couldn't play. Even though there was no official rule that prevented girls from playing football, everyone said that football was for boys only. The more people told her she couldn't play, the more she wanted to.

So she had started to drop by[1] Mr. Jackson's office daily, reminding him that there was no official rule that forbade her from trying out.

"I'm sorry, Mari, I really am," Mr. Jackson had told her, "but I just can't allow you to go out there against those bigger guys. They wouldn't take it easy on you. They'd be merciless, and you could get seriously hurt."

Even Jason, her best friend and a running back[2] on the team, had tried to talk her out of it.[3] "Why do you want to play football anyway?" he asked her. "You're the captain of the soccer team. You'll probably end up getting a scholarship. Why would you want to do something that could jeopardize[4] that?"

They were all good points, but Mari couldn't shake[5] her desire to play. She went to the soccer field one evening to work out some of her frustration. She had been out there at least an hour kicking ball after ball into an empty goal when the solution struck her so forcefully she stopped mid-kick. It was so obvious!

She could be the team's field goal kicker.[6]

FOOTNOTES

1 *drop by:* visit without warning
2 *running back:* a position on a football team
3 *talk her out of it:* convince her not to do it
4 *jeopardize:* put at risk
5 *shake:* get rid of
6 *field goal kicker:* person who kicks the ball through the goal posts

It was a position that she would be great at considering her kicking skills and experience, and she wouldn't really have to worry about getting hurt because hitting the kicker after the ball has been kicked is a penalty.

The next day she had knocked loudly on Mr. Jackson's door.

"Mari," Mr. Jackson said, as if he was neither surprised nor glad she was there.

"I've got it!" Mari had exclaimed. "I can be your field goal kicker!" She saw that he was about to object again, so she cut him off.[7] "Look, you know I'll be good at it, and it's the one position where I'll be the safest. Once I kick the ball, the other players aren't allowed to hit me, right?"

"Well, yes," Mr. Jackson began, "but if they get to you before you kick the ball, you're fair game."[8]

"It won't happen," Mari said. "Just give me a chance."

"It's different than kicking a soccer ball, Mari," Mr. Jackson said.

"I know that, but I can do it!" Mari had insisted. "Look, just come to my game tomorrow night and watch me kick. If you think I've got a chance, just let me try out."

The next Monday, Mari walked out onto the football field wearing practice pads that were too big for her and holding a helmet that smelled like vomit.

"Are you lost? This is football, not fútbol!"[9] Mitch Parrada, the quarterback,[10] teased.

"Yeah, go back to your fútbol practice and leave this sport to the guys!"

Mr. Jackson tried to quiet the team down, but the players mutinied, throwing more and more taunts her way.[11]

"You'd better watch out, I'm coming for you as soon as the ball is snapped!"

Mari tried to ignore them, but she couldn't concentrate; they looked evil and grotesque in their helmets and pads.

The snap came and the ball suddenly appeared under the holder's hand, waiting. It had happened too quickly, and her timing was off. She started her approach, but the defenders had already broken through the line and were coming for her. As she kicked the ball she saw it hit someone's outstretched hand at the same moment as she felt her leg hit something solid. They were upon her.

She felt her head snap back and her feet leave the ground, and she wondered if this was what it felt like for a ship to be capsized by a tsunami.

Suddenly it seemed like all of the oxygen had been sucked out of the air. She vaguely heard the coach's whistle and felt her aching leg and shoulder and neck and head, but nothing came close to the pain in her chest. She started to panic, thinking she would suffocate to death right there on the field. Mr. Jackson and Jason pushed through, dragging players off of her.

They helped her sit up and told her to breathe slowly.

"You had the wind knocked out of you,"[12] Jason said quietly. Mari heard Mr. Jackson telling everyone else to back off. One player muttered that she had gotten what she deserved. This brought her back with a snap, and she felt anger and determination swell within her. She was not going to let them beat her. She pushed Mr. Jackson and Jason back, stood up, and brushed her hands off.

"I get it now," she said. "I need to start a little sooner."

"You're crazy if you think I'm letting you do that again," Mr. Jackson said. "You're lucky you're even standing right now."

Mari stared at him and calmly, slowly said, "I can do it. One more chance."

Mr. Jackson looked back for a moment, shook his head and signaled for them to line up again. Mari heard some laughter from the guys on the team, and it made her insides harden.[13]

This time when they lined up she paid attention to nothing but the spot on the ground where the football would be waiting. She saw the snap, and before the ball was even in place began taking her measured steps towards it. She planted her right foot and felt her left foot swinging through the air. This time the ball spiraled up end over end, clear of the reaching arms of the other players. They stopped struggling to get at her and turned to watch. . . .

As Mari trudged back up the hill to the locker room, holding her helmet in her hand and picking the grass off her pants, she was too tired to even smile as she replayed in her mind what Mr. Jackson had told her before she left.

"We'll see you tomorrow at practice. You made the team."

FOOTNOTES

[12] *had the wind knocked out of you:* lost your breath after being hit

[13] *insides harden:* feel more determined

11

Explain Yourself

Answer each question on a separate piece of paper. Be sure to explain your answers.

1. What two exercises might you do **simultaneously**? Why?

2. What would happen if germs **pervaded** your house? Explain.

3. Have your friends ever seemed **merciless** to you? Explain.

4. Has your hair ever **mutinied** against you? Explain.

5. What **grotesque** things might you find in a refrigerator? Explain.

6. What would you do if you were on a boat that **capsized**? Explain.

7. What might you have a **vague** memory of? Explain.

8. What might you walk through that would cause you to **trudge**? Why?

9. How would you feel if somebody **ravaged** your science project? Why?

10. Do you think all heroes and heroines are **stalwart**? Why or why not?

simultaneously When things happen simultaneously, they happen at the same time.

pervade If something pervades an area, it spreads throughout.

merciless When you are merciless, you act cruelly and show no concern, pity, or mercy.

mutiny If you mutiny, you rebel against your leader or whoever is in charge.

grotesque If you think something looks grotesque, it looks so strange that it disturbs you.

capsize If a boat is capsized, it is turned over.

vague When something is vague, it is so unclear that it is hard to understand.

trudge When you trudge, you walk with slow, heavy steps.

ravage When something is ravaged, it is so badly damaged that it is destroyed.

stalwart If you are stalwart, people can depend on you to be loyal and hard working.

Take It Further

Complete these sentences on a separate piece of paper.

1. We watched as the waitress **simultaneously** . . .

2. One thing I never expected to **pervade** our class was . . .

3. The freed lion **mercilessly** . . .

4. On our family vacation, my brother and I **mutinied** by . . .

5. Patrick thought the pictures looked **grotesque** because . . .

6. Stephania's rowboat **capsized** when she . . .

7. Because the directions for building the bike ramp were so **vague**, . . .

8. I **trudged** to the dinner table because I knew . . .

9. Jawaad's bike was **ravaged** after . . .

10. My friend Amy proved that she was **stalwart** when she . . .

Explore It

You know that adding a suffix to the end of a word can change its meaning and part of speech. Did you realize that *merciless* contains a suffix? So does its opposite, *merciful*.

Someone who is merciful is full of mercy, or kindness and sympathy, for others. Someone who is merciless does not have mercy for others.

In a small group, act out a quick skit about the situation your teacher describes. At least two people in your group should be actors, and one person should be the director. When the actors begin the skit, the director should call out "merciful" or "merciless." The actors should change their character's behavior based on the director's instructions—they should act merciful or merciless based on what the director says. Remember, the director can change his or her mind at any time during the skit!

VANISHED LANDS

Atlantis

You've heard of a boat capsizing, but can the sea swallow a whole civilization? That's what might have happened to the island of Atlantis. According to an ancient Greek legend, earthquakes caused the entire island and its people to sink to the bottom of the ocean. The story of Atlantis may be a myth, but some people are still searching for this mysterious underwater land.

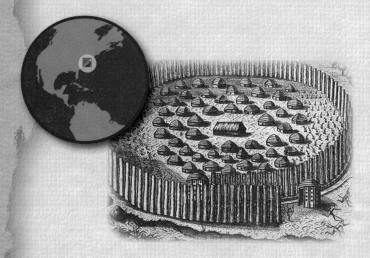

Roanoke

When the English built a town called Roanoke in North America in 1587, they didn't know what its fate would be. By 1590, all the people and houses in Roanoke had vanished! No one was found—dead or alive. Were the people of Roanoke mercilessly killed? Did they join a Native American tribe? To this day, nobody knows what happened.

Pompeii

In AD 79, a volcano called Mount Vesuvius erupted and destroyed the Roman city of Pompeii. Lava, gas, and ashes pervaded the city, and Pompeii lay buried for hundreds of years. Finally, in the 19th century, an archaeologist discovered Pompeii's underground ruins. He also made a grotesque discovery: some of the holes in the ground around Pompeii were shaped like the bodies of the people who had died there.

Machu Picchu

A young college professor traveling in South America discovers a lost city that was home to an ancient civilization. Sound like a good movie? In this case, it's true! Machu Picchu was built by the Incan people in the area that is now known as Peru. It was a royal estate for Incan rulers. After Machu Picchu was abandoned, the magnificent city remained untouched for more than 500 years.

Dwarka

Legends describe how a giant wave ravaged and swept away the Indian city of Dwarka. For years, many thought this story was nothing more than a myth. In the 1980s, scientists discovered an underwater city that could be the city from the legend! The world's first underwater museum might be built near modern-day Dwarka so that visitors can explore the drowned ruins.

Rev Up Your Writing

You've just read about several lost cities and civilizations. Are you fascinated by lost civilizations? Why or why not? Write about which lost land you would most like to discover. Use as many of the vocabulary words as possible but make sense.

Word Organizer

Copy this graphic organizer onto a separate piece of paper.

Think of words that describe the word *grotesque* and write your answers in the ovals. Then give examples of things that are grotesque and write your answers in the boxes. Explain your answers.

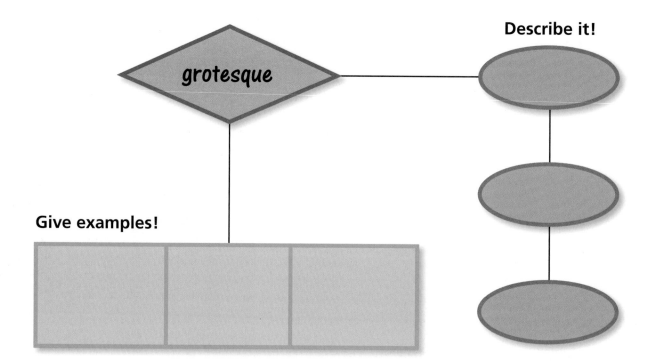

Mmmm... RATS!

You may have heard of Magellan's famous trip around the world, but have you heard about the difficulties the sailors faced? Nobody had sailed around the world before, so nobody really knew how big it was, which way to go, or how much food to bring. Before the explorers even got halfway, some of the sailors tried to mutiny, and then the whole expedition ran out of food! To survive, the sailors had to eat worm-infested biscuit crumbs—the leftovers from what the rats had eaten. When the crumbs were gone, the sailors ate sawdust, leather straps, and even started catching and eating the rats! Only 18 of the nearly 300 crew members survived to make it back home.

How to SURVIVE in the Wilderness

You've left the campsite, and suddenly you find yourself turned around. You're lost! Surely a search party will come to look for you, but what should you do until then?

- ⊙ **Stay where you are.** People will trudge through every inch of the forest until they find you. Trying to find your own way back may actually take you farther away from the rescue crew.

- ⊙ **Find shelter.** Being exposed to the weather is often one of the most dangerous parts of being lost. Find a place that is warm and dry.

- ⊙ **Attract attention.** Always carry a brightly colored object, such as an extra shirt, a hat, or a bandana. Lay it out in the open where search teams can find it.

- ⊙ **Drink.** Dehydration, or lack of water, is one of the biggest dangers of being lost. Drink from a stream if you have to, even if the water is not crystal clear. The dirty water might save your life!

- ⊙ **Stick together.** If you get lost with someone else, don't wander away from each other. Two heads are always better than one.

BASHER Five-Two

He survived an exploding jet and a high-speed fall through the air. He trudged through the wilderness for six days. When he ran out of food, he ate leaves and ants. When he ran out of water, he drank rainwater from his wet socks. In *Basher Five-Two,* Scott O'Grady, a stalwart fighter pilot shot down by enemies during a war, tells his thrilling story of bravery and survival.

While the first few chapters are a bit difficult because of O'Grady's use of vague piloting terms, the rest of the book moves smoothly. You may even find yourself learning a bit about wilderness survival and aviation along the way!

Simultaneously thought-provoking and awe-inspiring, *Basher Five-Two* promises to be one of the top nonfiction adventure books of the decade.

Rev Up Your Writing

These stories are about people eating and drinking disgusting things to survive. Sometimes a situation requires us to try things we wouldn't normally do. Write about such a time in your own life or the life of someone you know. Use as many of the vocabulary words as possible but make sense.

Can You Relate?

Copy this graphic organizer onto a separate piece of paper. Match the following words with their related vocabulary word. If a word relates to more than one vocabulary word, explain why.

fidelity   Someone who shows fidelity supports his or her friends.

mettle   A person who has mettle is brave and willing to do daring things.

sabotage   If you sabotage something, you destroy it or stop it from working.

staunch   A staunch person will work on a task until it is finished.

usurp   If you usurp someone's position, you take it over.

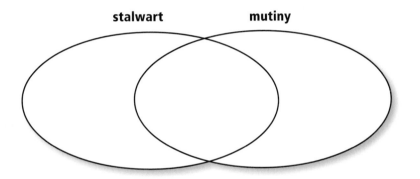

stalwart   **mutiny**

In Your Own Words

Respond to one of the following prompts on a separate piece of paper. As you respond, use as many of the vocabulary words as possible. Be creative but make sense!

▶ Write about a time when you or someone you know faced an unusual problem. What was the problem? How did you solve it?

▶ Write an adventure story about a group of explorers setting off on a new adventure. Try writing your story from a strange or surprising point of view.

▶ Write about a topic of your choice.

VOCABULARY

simultaneously
pervade
merciless
mutiny
grotesque
capsize
vague
trudge
ravage
stalwart

The **Struggle** to Be an All-American Girl

By Elizabeth Wong
Illustrated by
Fred Willingham

Caught between two different cultures, Elizabeth Wong—a Chinese American—describes her childhood struggle with all things related to her Chinese heritage.

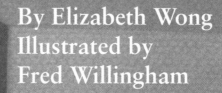

It's still there, the Chinese school on Yale Street where my brother and I used to go. Despite the new coat of paint and the high wire fence, the school I knew ten years ago remains remarkably, stoically the same.

Every day at 5 P.M., instead of playing with our fourth- and fifth-grade friends or sneaking out to the empty lot to hunt ghosts and animal bones, my brother and I had to go to Chinese school. No amount of kicking, screaming, or pleading could dissuade my mother, who was solidly determined to have us learn the language of our heritage.

Forcibly, she walked us the seven long, hilly blocks from our home to school, depositing our defiant, tearful faces before the stern principal. My only memory of him is that he swayed on his heels like a palm tree, and he always clasped his impatient, twitching hands behind his back. I recognized him as a repressed maniacal child killer and knew that if we ever saw his hands we'd be in big trouble.

We all sat in little chairs in an empty auditorium. The room smelled like Chinese medicine, an imported faraway mustiness. Like ancient mothballs[1] or dirty closets. I hated that smell. I favored crisp new scents. Like the soft French perfume that my American teacher wore in public school.

There was a stage far to the right, flanked by an American flag and the flag of the Nationalist Republic of China, which was also red, white, and blue but not as pretty.

Although the emphasis at the school was mainly language—speaking, reading, writing—the lessons always began with an exercise in politeness. With the entrance of the teacher, the best student would tap a bell and everyone would get up, kowtow,[2] and chant, "Sing san ho," the phonetic for "How are you, teacher?"

Being ten years old, I had better things to learn than ideographs[3] copied painstakingly in lines that ran right to left from the tip of a *moc but*, a real ink pen that had to be held in an awkward way if blotches were to be avoided. After all, I could do the multiplication tables, name the satellites of Mars, and write reports on *Little Women* and *Black Beauty*. Nancy Drew, my favorite book heroine, never spoke Chinese.

FOOTNOTES

[1] *mothballs:* small balls of chemicals used to protect clothing from moths
[2] *kowtow:* a Chinese custom that involves kneeling and touching the forehead to the ground to show respect
[3] *ideographs:* symbols used to represent words

The language was a source of embarrassment. More times than not, I had tried to disassociate myself from the nagging loud voice that followed me wherever I wandered in the nearby American supermarket outside Chinatown. The voice belonged to my grandmother, a fragile woman in her seventies who could outshout the best of the street vendors. Her humor was raunchy, her Chinese rhythmless, patternless. It was quick, it was loud, it was unbeautiful. It was not like the quiet, lilting romance of French or the gentle refinement of the American South. Chinese sounded pedestrian. Public.

In Chinatown, the comings and goings of hundreds of Chinese on their daily tasks sounded chaotic and frenzied. I did not want to be thought of as mad, as talking gibberish. When I spoke English, people nodded at me, smiled sweetly, said encouraging words. Even the people in my culture would cluck and say that I'd do well in life. "My, doesn't she move her lips fast," they would say, meaning that I'd be able to keep up with the world outside Chinatown.

My brother was even more fanatical than I about speaking English. He was especially hard on my mother, criticizing her, often cruelly, for her pidgin speech[4]—smatterings[5] of Chinese scattered like chop suey[6] in her conversation. "It's not 'what it is,' Mom," he'd say in exasperation. "It's 'What *is* it, what *is* it, what *is* it!'" Sometimes Mom might leave out an occasional "the" or "a," or perhaps a verb of being. He would stop her in midsentence: "Say it again, Mom. Say it right." When he tripped over his own tongue,[7] he'd blame it on her: "See, Mom, it's all your fault. You set a bad example."

FOOTNOTES

[4] *pidgin speech:* speech made up of two or more languages

[5] *smatterings:* small amounts

[6] *chop suey:* a Chinese-American dish

[7] *tripped over his own tongue:* had trouble speaking

What infuriated my mother most was when my brother cornered her on her consonants, especially "r." My father had played a cruel joke on Mom by assigning her an American name that her tongue wouldn't allow her to say. No matter how hard she tried, "Ruth" always ended up "Luth" or "Roof."

After two years of writing with a *moc but* and reciting words with multiples of meanings, I finally was granted a cultural divorce. I was permitted to stop Chinese school.

I thought of myself as multicultural. I preferred tacos to egg rolls; I enjoyed Cinco de Mayo[8] more than Chinese New Year.

At last, I was one of you; I wasn't one of them.

Sadly, I still am.

FOOTNOTES
[8] *Cinco de Mayo:* a Mexican holiday celebrated on May 5

Explain Yourself

VOCABULARY

Answer each question on a separate piece of paper. Be sure to explain your answers.

1. If your parents assigned you a lot of chores, would you remain **stoic**? Explain.

2. When might you find it hard to **repress** your emotions? Explain.

3. Would you describe your best friend as a **maniacal** person? Why or why not?

4. What is a task that you would do **painstakingly**? Why?

5. Would it bother you if your teacher had a **lilting** voice? Explain.

6. Would you expect young children to show **refinement**? Why or why not?

7. Would you consider eating cereal for breakfast to be **pedestrian**? Explain.

8. How would you deal with someone who **infuriates** you? Explain.

9. What would happen if you spoke to your teacher in a **condescending** way? Why?

10. Would you feel **contrite** if you were chosen to play on the school soccer team and your best friend wasn't? Explain.

stoic   A stoic person doesn't show any emotion, even when bad things happen.

repress   If you repress a feeling, you hold it back or keep it inside.

maniacal   When you act maniacal, you act wild and crazy, like a maniac.

painstakingly   When you do something painstakingly, you do it very slowly and carefully.

lilting   If a sound is lilting, it is pleasantly light and musical.

refinement   If you show refinement, you act politely and show good taste.

pedestrian   Something that is pedestrian is so common and ordinary that it is not interesting.

infuriate   When someone or something infuriates you, it makes you extremely angry, even furious.

condescending   When you are condescending to others, you talk down to them, making them feel unimportant or stupid.

contrite   If you are contrite, you are very sorry or ashamed.

Take It Further

Complete these sentences on a separate piece of paper.

1. James could not remain **stoic** after he . . .

2. Amelia **repressed** her anger when . . .

3. The bus driver instantly became **maniacal** when . . .

4. When Ivan went to the hospital, the doctor **painstakingly** . . .

5. The professional football player's **lilting** voice surprised me because . . .

6. I was surprised when my brother acted with **refinement** because . . .

7. Mary's trip to the zoo was **pedestrian** until . . .

8. It always **infuriates** me when my friends . . .

9. Elena was being **condescending** when she said . . .

10. I didn't feel **contrite** after arguing with my friend because . . .

Explore It

Words often have more than one meaning. For example, _pedestrian_ can mean "ordinary" or "someone who travels on foot."

pedestrian = ordinary
Many of today's movies seem to be dull and boring. The same plots are repeated over and over again with different actors and actresses in the lead roles. When you see a movie that you find boring and ordinary, you can describe it as pedestrian.

> Imagine that you have been hired to write a movie script, and your boss wants the movie's plot to be interesting. What things would you do to make sure the plot is not pedestrian? Write a summary of the movie you would write.

pedestrian = someone who travels on foot
When you drive down a city street, you may see many people walking. People who travel on foot are called pedestrians.

> Describe a time when you were a pedestrian and something unusual happened to you. Would the event have affected you if you had not been a pedestrian? Why or why not?

BEASTLY INVENTIONS

The Internet, cell phones, and DVD players are practical inventions that have improved people's lives. Some inventions, however, are just wacky. Many of the world's craziest inventions were created for animals or for people who love animals.

Secret Language of Dogs?

Woof! Grr! Have you ever wondered what a dog was trying to say with its bark? Now you don't have to wonder. A Japanese company has created a bark translator. The device analyzes your dog's bark and displays a text message letting you know just how the dog feels. Even if a dog wanted to repress its emotions, it couldn't.

Car Wash for Pets?

Anyone who has owned a pet knows that bath time can be a horrible experience. It's funny how soap and water can turn the most well behaved animal into a maniacal beast! Well, the Pet Shower was invented to make bathing pets an enjoyable experience—at least for the owner. No more struggling with a wet, infuriated pet! That's because the pet's body is enclosed in the shower. Once the animal is in the shower, it cannot escape. However, owners may want to stand back once their pets are free!

What a Spectacle!

A chicken wearing eyeglasses would not be a very pedestrian sight. But in 1903, a man named Andrew Jackson invented a pair of spectacles for chickens. Why would a chicken need eyeglasses? Although it's hard to believe, the glasses were not used to correct the bird's vision. Instead, the glasses were used to prevent the chickens' eyes from being pecked by other chickens!

Rodent Workout

It's not easy to take small animals, such as mice and gerbils, out in public. Not everyone welcomes these furry creatures. But if you owned a Gerbil Shirt, you would no longer have to repress those feelings of regret over leaving your fur ball at home. The Gerbil Shirt is a series of tubes that wrap around a person. Mice or gerbils can make themselves at home inside the tubes so they can run around and get exercise. The animals have plenty of air and room to roam. Just don't make any sudden movements or fall down!

Artificial Affection

In today's busy world, many pet owners do not have the time to give their pets the attention they need. That's where the Pet Petter comes in. This device has a mechanical petting arm with a human-like hand attached to the end. Pet owners no longer have to feel contrite about not having the time to show affection to their pets.

Rev Up Your Writing

These are just a few examples of unusual inventions for pets. Write about a strange invention that you would create. What is your invention used for? What makes it strange? Use as many of the vocabulary words as possible but make sense.

Word Organizer

Copy this graphic organizer onto a separate piece of paper.

List things that might infuriate a teacher and write your answers under the teacher column. Then list things that might infuriate a student and write your answers under the student column. Explain your answers.

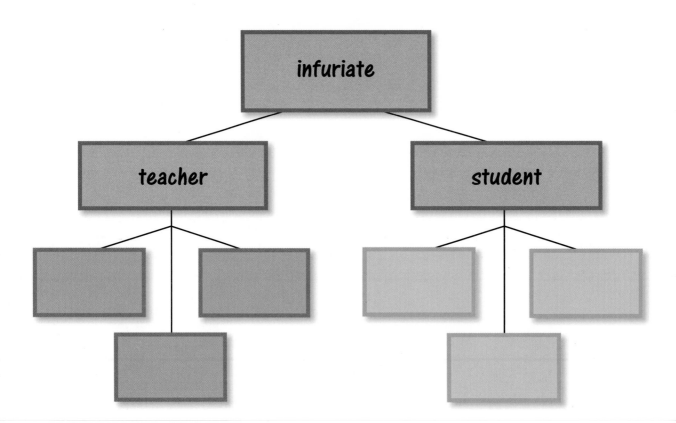

Paging Dr. America

Got a question about something you've seen on your adventures? Well, Dr. America—our expert on the country's most unusual events—is here to help!

Q

Dear Dr. America,

I was in Colorado this October enjoying the quiet, lilting sounds of the outdoors when all of a sudden I heard strange, loud noises. A herd of gorillas was running down the street! I was so frightened that I ran away! Why do they let gorillas run wild in Colorado?

—Going Ape

A

Dear Going Ape,
Gorillas may live in Colorado zoos, but they don't roam the streets. What you witnessed was the Denver Gorilla Run. It's a race in which each runner dresses up in a gorilla costume. They run to raise money for endangered gorillas. There was nothing to fear!

—Dr. America

Q

Dear Dr. America,

As I was traveling in the Midwest, I saw signs advertising a lawn mower race. I thought I was seeing things, but then I saw more signs. Am I going crazy?

—Seeing Things

A

Dear Seeing Things,
You aren't going crazy. What you saw were signs for lawn mower drag racing. The rules are simple. Stoic drivers race their mowers down a marked course, sometimes reaching speeds of 127 mph. Whoever crosses the finish line first wins.

—Dr. America

Q

Dear Dr. America,

Last September I traveled to Nevada. As I was driving through the desert, I saw several crazy people riding on camels with thousands of people watching them. What could they possibly be doing? It looked like a waste of time to me.

—Camel Spotter

A

Dear Camel Spotter,

Don't be so condescending! The people on the camels weren't crazy. They were just taking part in the International Camel Race, which takes place each year in Virginia City, Nevada. About 27 jockeys enter the race and try to get the camels to run. This isn't easy because camels have a short attention span and can be quite unpredictable!

—Dr. America

Q

Dear Dr. America,

As I was visiting South Hill Mall in Puyallup, Washington, I was almost run over by five men pushing a bed through the parking lot in a mad rush! At first I thought they were a bunch of unrefined, maniacal deliverymen, but now I'm not so sure. Help!

—Nearly Run Over

A

Dear Nearly Run Over,

I can help! Each year the people of Puyallup hold the "Daffodil 200" bed race. In this race, five team members struggle to balance a wrought-iron bed on wheels. A rider lies in the middle of the bed as the racers push the bed around the parking lot of the mall. Teams work painstakingly to make sure that their beds are in the best racing condition. The race raises money for the community float, which is displayed in the San Diego Holiday Bowl Parade.

—Dr. America

Rev Up Your Writing

You've read about some unusual events that take place in the United States. Now describe an unusual event that you've seen or heard about. What makes this event unusual? What is the purpose for the event? Use as many of the vocabulary words as possible but make sense.

Can You Relate?

Copy this graphic organizer onto a separate piece of paper. Match the following words with their related vocabulary word. If a word relates to more than one vocabulary word, explain why.

decorum When you show decorum, you behave in a correct, respectable way.

dissonant If something is described as dissonant, it has unpleasant, harsh sounds.

eccentric An eccentric person behaves in a way that others consider strange and unusual.

obstreperous If you are obstreperous, you are noisy and out of control.

vociferous If you are vociferous, you speak loudly to make sure that you are heard.

lilting	maniacal	refinement

In Your Own Words

Respond to one of the following prompts on a separate piece of paper. As you respond, use as many of the vocabulary words as possible. Be creative but make sense!

▶ Write about a time when you or a friend experienced another culture's traditions or customs. How were the traditions different from your own? What did you learn from this experience?

▶ Think about an invention that has changed your life in either a positive or negative way. Write a letter to the inventor. Describe how the invention has affected you and why.

▶ Write about a topic of your choice.

VOCABULARY

stoic
repress
maniacal
painstakingly
lilting
refinement
pedestrian
infuriate
condescending
contrite

Memories of Our Fathers

Can a father change the way you see the world? Can he change the way you see yourself? In these two poems, the speakers search for answers as they remember their fathers.

Illustrated by Durga Bernhard and Jared Montano

My Father Is a Simple Man
By Luis Omar Salinas

I walk to town with my father
to buy a newspaper. He walks slower
than I do so I must slow up.
The street is filled with children.
We argue about the price
of pomegranates,[1] I convince
him it is the fruit of scholars.
He has taken me on this journey
and it's been lifelong.
He's sure I'll be healthy
so long as I eat more oranges,
and tells me the orange
has seeds and so is perpetual;
and we too will come back
like the orange trees.
I ask him what he thinks
about death and he says
he will gladly face it when
it comes but won't jump
out in front of a car.
I'd gladly give my life[2]
for this man with a sixth
grade education, whose kindness
and patience are true . . .

FOOTNOTES
[1] *pomegranates:* small, red fruits
[2] *give my life:* die

Continued on page 34

The truth of it is, he's the scholar,
and when the bitter-hard reality
comes at me like a punishing
evil stranger, I can always
remember that here was a man
who was a worker and provider,
who learned the simple facts
in life and lived by them,
who held no pretense.
And when he leaves without
benefit of fanfare or applause
I shall have learned what little
there is about greatness.

I Remember My Father's Hands

By Lisa Suhair Majaj

Because they were large, and square,
fingers chunky, black hair like wire

because they fingered worry beads over and over
(that muted clicking, that constant motion, that secular prayer)

because they ripped bread with quiet purpose,
dipped fresh green oil like a birthright[3]

because after his mother's funeral they raised a tea cup,
set it down untouched, uncontrollably trembling

because when they trimmed hedges, pruned roses,
their tenderness caught my breath with jealousy

because once when I was a child they cupped[4] my face,
dry and warm, flesh full and calloused, for a long moment

because over his wife's still form they faltered[5]
great mute helpless beasts

because when his own lungs filled and sank they reached out
for the first time pleading

because when I look at my hands
his own speak back

FOOTNOTES

[3] *birthright:* a right
someone has from birth

[4] *cupped:* held with
both hands

[5] *faltered:* moved
unsteadily

Explain Yourself

VOCABULARY

Answer each question on a separate piece of paper. Be sure to explain your answers.

1. Why might you give a friend a **pretense**?

2. Whose arrival at your school might cause a lot of **fanfare**? Why?

3. What type of event would you wear **muted** colors to?

4. Which is more likely to be **secular**, a temple or an ice cream shop? Why?

5. What might make your hands **calloused**? Explain.

6. What things from last year do you **reminisce** about?

7. If you have **adulation** for someone, would you want to talk to that person? Why or why not?

8. If your grade on an exam was **laudable**, would your parents be upset with you? Explain.

9. Who would you want to **emulate**? Explain.

10. What might a villain **exemplify**?

pretense   A pretense is something you do or say to make people believe something that is not true.

fanfare   Fanfare is music or a showy display celebrating someone or something important.

muted   Muted colors and sounds are gentle and soft, not strong and bright.

secular   If something is secular, it has nothing to do with religion.

callous   If something is callous, it is thick skinned or insensitive.

reminisce   When you reminisce, you think back on good things from the past that you miss.

adulation   Adulation is a feeling of deep admiration or worship.

laudable   If something is laudable, it is so good it deserves to be praised or rewarded.

emulate   If you emulate someone, you try to be like that person because you admire him or her.

exemplify   If you exemplify something, you are an outstanding example of it.

Take It Further

Complete these sentences on a separate piece of paper.

1. We knew Jerry was putting on a **pretense** when he . . .

2. There was a lot of **fanfare** when . . .

3. Stephanie liked the **muted** sound of . . .

4. Akira says that her favorite **secular** holiday is . . .

5. George's feet became **calloused** after he . . .

6. Sierra likes to listen to her grandmother **reminisce** about . . .

7. My best friend deserves **adulation** because . . .

8. Jamal did something **laudable** for his sister when he . . .

9. The kinds of people I try to **emulate** are . . .

10. Shelby **exemplified** being an older sibling by . . .

Explore It

The words *emulate*, "to be like someone you admire" and *imitate* "to copy what a person says or does" are often confused with each other because they have similar meanings and they also sound alike. But, they are very different words. The word *emulate* has a positive meaning, while the word *imitate* can have both positive and negative meaning. You might imitate the actions of someone you admire, but sometimes people imitate others to be funny or to make fun of them.

Working in a group, make up a skit where someone does something that others would want to emulate. Have the rest of the group emulate that person's behavior. Then, have another person do something funny that others would want to imitate and have the rest of the group imitate that person.

Yep, That's a Building!

If you wanted to explain to someone what buildings look like, what would you say? You might explain that buildings have doors and windows, a rectangular shape, and muted colors. Some are one-story houses and some are soaring skyscrapers, but most of them have similar features. However, some very creative people have come up with some pretty crazy building designs. Whether it's a church that resembles a sandcastle, or a secular structure shaped like a pineapple, some buildings are just plain weird!

Margate, New Jersey is home to the world's largest elephant building. In 1881 James Lafferty built this 56-foot-tall building and named it Lucy. The building weighs 90 tons and is six stories high. Visitors can walk up the staircase inside Lucy's legs and sit on Lucy's back.

A man from Zillah, Washington held no pretense about his disapproval of a political disgrace involving bribery and the use of an oil field named Teapot Dome. In 1922, he built his gas station in the shape of a giant teapot as a sign of protest.

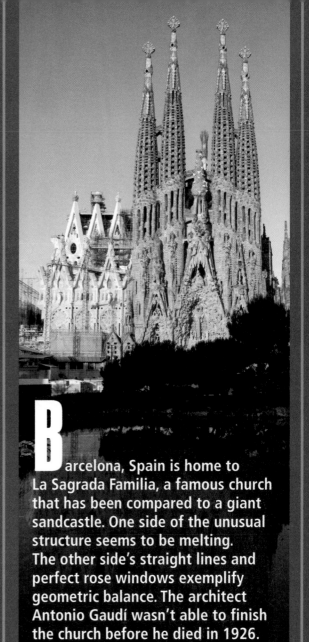

B arcelona, Spain is home to La Sagrada Familia, a famous church that has been compared to a giant sandcastle. One side of the unusual structure seems to be melting. The other side's straight lines and perfect rose windows exemplify geometric balance. The architect Antonio Gaudí wasn't able to finish the church before he died in 1926.

T he Big Pineapple brings visitors from all around the world to visit Sunshine Plantation in Queensland, Australia. The building has an observation deck at the top, and the inside contains a museum where people can reminisce about the early days of the plantation.

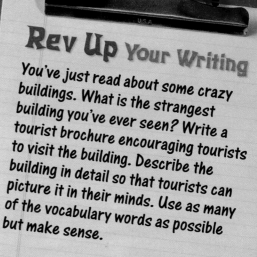

Rev Up Your Writing

You've just read about some crazy buildings. What is the strangest building you've ever seen? Write a tourist brochure encouraging tourists to visit the building. Describe the building in detail so that tourists can picture it in their minds. Use as many of the vocabulary words as possible but make sense.

Word Organizer

Copy this graphic organizer onto a separate piece of paper.

Think of words that describe a person who treats others callously and write your answers in the ovals. Then give examples of things that a callous person might do and write your answers in the boxes. Explain your answers.

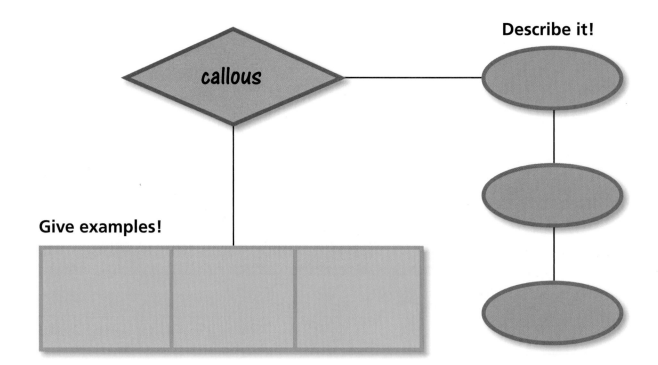

Dee McGreevey: Detective

The name of Dee McGreevey was well known around the town.
If anything was missing, she'd make sure that it was found.
The laudable detective never failed in any quest.
When hunting stolen items, there's no doubt she was the best.

Anytime the cops were stumped, they'd call in you-know-who.
In came Dee McGreevey, and—presto!—she'd find a clue.
Callous thieves and robbers stood no chance against this woman.
She'd track down every bad guy and stop every evil plan.

Nobody could stop her once McGreevey got a hunch.
She'd find some missing diamonds and be home in time for lunch.
From missing cash to stolen pearls, Dee solved every case.
She earned folks' adulation with a smile on her face.

Now the neighbors saw McGreevey standing by her door.
She looked like she'd been standing there three hours, maybe more.
She'd certainly like to enter; it would really be a breeze.
If she could only figure out where she had put her keys.

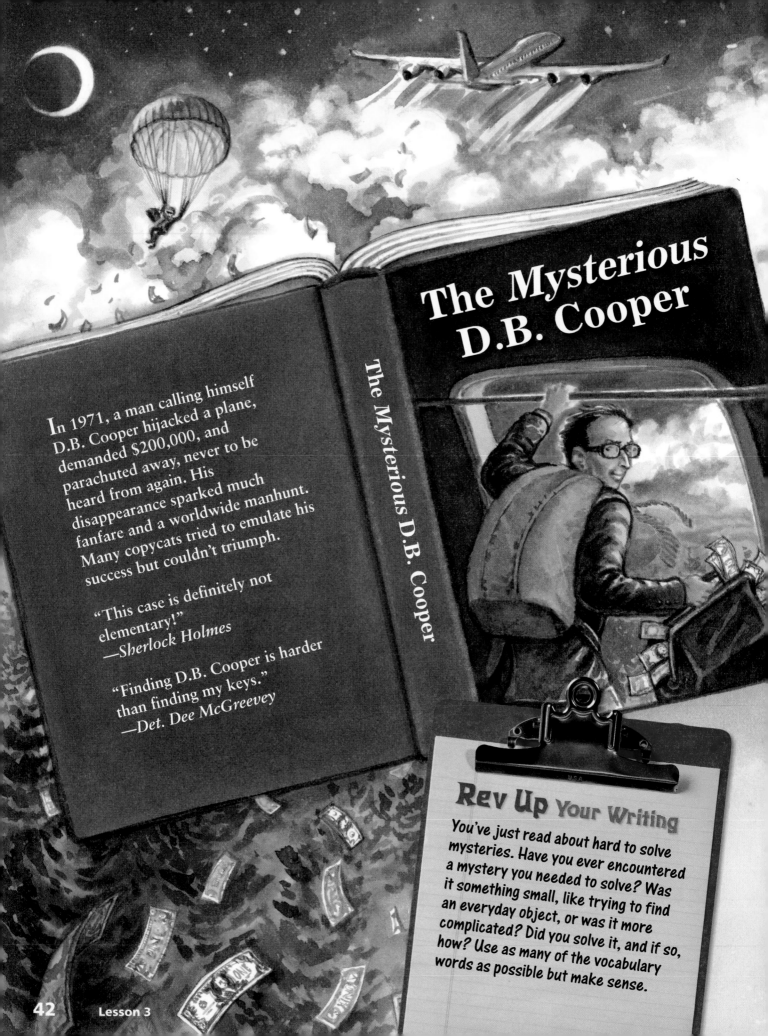

The Mysterious D.B. Cooper

In 1971, a man calling himself D.B. Cooper hijacked a plane, demanded $200,000, and parachuted away, never to be heard from again. His disappearance sparked much fanfare and a worldwide manhunt. Many copycats tried to emulate his success but couldn't triumph.

"This case is definitely not elementary!"
—Sherlock Holmes

"Finding D.B. Cooper is harder than finding my keys."
—Det. Dee McGreevey

The Mysterious D.B. Cooper

Rev Up Your Writing

You've just read about hard to solve mysteries. Have you ever encountered a mystery you needed to solve? Was it something small, like trying to find an everyday object, or was it more complicated? Did you solve it, and if so, how? Use as many of the vocabulary words as possible but make sense.

Can You Relate?

Copy this graphic organizer onto a separate piece of paper. Match the following words with their related vocabulary word. If a word relates to more than one vocabulary word, explain why.

archetype   An archetype is a model example of something.

embodiment   If someone is the embodiment of fairness, that person is fair in everything he or she does.

feign   If you feign happiness, you pretend to be happy.

poseur   A poseur is the best example of a person who puts on an act to impress others.

prevaricate   If you prevaricate, you don't tell the truth.

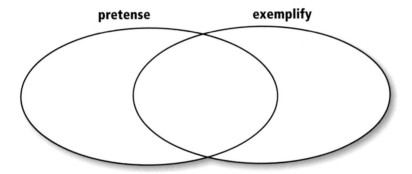

pretense   exemplify

In Your Own Words

Respond to one of the following prompts on a separate piece of paper. As you respond, use as many of the vocabulary words as possible. Be creative but make sense!

▶ Describe the sights and sounds you experienced on your way to school this morning. How did these things make you feel about the day?

▶ Imagine that you had the chance to visit your favorite celebrity for a day. Write a letter to a friend that describes your day. Explain what you did during the visit and describe your impression of the celebrity.

▶ Write about a topic of your choice.

VOCABULARY

pretense
fanfare
muted
secular
callous
reminisce
adulation
laudable
emulate
exemplify

43

The Tiger's Whisker

Retold by An Wei Chi
Illustrated by Lin Wang

Yun Ok's husband has completely changed after coming home from war. Yun Ok decides to make a potion that will cure her husband, but getting the main ingredient might cost Yun Ok her life.

*M*any years ago in Korea, there lived a young woman named Yun Ok. Her husband had recently returned from war, and although Yun Ok was happy to see him, she found that he had changed and was no longer the man she remembered. He was miserable and became easily irritated. As time passed, Yun Ok became equally unhappy.

Searching for a solution, Yun Ok made a long trip up a mountain to where a venerable sage[1] lived as a hermit. This sage was famous for his curative potions,[2] and Yun Ok hoped that he would help her. Unfortunately, the sage was not quick to offer a solution.

"Why are you here?" he inquired in an angry tone.

"Oh renowned sage," said Yun Ok, "Please make me a potion."

"What for?" asked the sage.

"I love my husband very much, but he has recently returned from war, and he is a very different man. He used to be so kind and gentle. Now he is angry and depressed. He ignores me or yells at me, and there seems to be nothing I can do to make him happy. He is indifferent to his work, and most of the time he simply stares at the ground and acts as if I do not exist.

"War has destroyed many good men. I cannot change that," the hermit replied.

"Please take pity on us and give me a potion that will bring my loving husband back to me."

"It's not that easy," said the sage. "Leave me alone and I will contemplate your ordeal. Come back in a few days."

When Yun Ok returned, the sage explained that he was willing to help her but that a potion would require one essential ingredient: a whisker plucked from a living tiger. Yun Ok would have to bring the tiger's whisker to the sage.

"How can I get a tiger's whisker?" Yun Ok exclaimed incredulously.

"That is your problem, not mine," said the sage. "If you care about this matter, you will get it." With that, the sage turned his back on Yun Ok and refused to speak to her again until she returned with the whisker.

FOOTNOTES
[1] *sage:* very wise person
[2] *curative potions:* medicines

Yun Ok was devastated. She had no idea how she could get a tiger's whisker. She pondered the issue long and hard over the next few weeks. She knew there was a tiger's den on the side of a mountain, not far from the hermit's home. But how could she get close enough to a tiger to pluck a whisker without getting herself killed?

Her husband seemed to be getting worse and worse, so Yun Ok decided it was time for her to make her move. She surreptitiously crept to the kitchen one night, prepared a bowl of meat and rice, and headed for the mountain. She slowly climbed to the cave, calling out to the tiger. Hearing her call, the tiger hissed and growled. In fear, Yun Ok left the food on the ground and ran home.

The next night Yun Ok returned up the mountain with more meat and rice. The tiger snarled as Yun Ok approached his den. Yun Ok returned the following night, too. Each night she left the meat and rice for the tiger and moved closer to the den. After a while, the tiger became accustomed to Yun Ok's delicious food and soft steps.

One night, as Yun Ok made her way up the mountain, she saw glowing eyes up ahead on the trail. She was scared, but slowly bent down and offered the food to the tiger, showing the tiger that she meant no harm. Soon the tiger met her on the trail. They began to observe each other in silence. A short time later, Yun Ok began to talk calmly and softly to the tiger. Within a few months the tiger began to eat out of Yun Ok's hands, and Yun Ok began to pet the tiger lovingly on the head as the tiger purred.

Six months passed and Yun Ok finally built up the courage to make her request. She asked the tiger for a whisker.

The tiger expressed his agreement by lying before Yun Ok as she plucked a single whisker from his face. Then they parted.

In her excitement, Yun Ok ran directly to the house of the sage.

"I got it!" she cried as she knocked excitedly on the hermit's door. "I have the tiger's whisker!"

The sage slowly opened the door and seized the whisker from Yun Ok. He quickly ascertained that it was a real tiger's whisker. Then he threw the whisker into his fireplace where it caught fire and burned.

"Why did you do that?" Yun Ok yelled.

"How did you get that whisker?" the sage asked.

Yun Ok explained, "Every night I sneaked out of my house and climbed the mountain to the tiger's den. I slowly approached the den, each night moving closer to the tiger. I gave the tiger the finest meat I could prepare and talked soothingly. With time I gained the tiger's trust and affection. I was finally able to get the whisker from the tiger. And now it is gone."

The sage laughed while summarizing Yun Ok's story, "So, you were able to calm a wild beast and gain its affection."

"Yes I did," Yun Ok replied in a huff. "A lot of good that did. You threw the whisker into the fire, and now I will have no cure for my husband."

"You don't need a whisker to cure your husband" the hermit claimed. "Are you more afraid of your husband than you are of a savage beast? Don't you think your husband will respond to the same patience and kindness that you offered the tiger? Go home and give your husband the same affection that you have given that tiger."

Yun Ok reflected on[3] the sage's advice as she walked back to her home, where she found her husband waiting.

FOOTNOTES

[3] *reflected on:* thought about

Explain Yourself

VOCABULARY

Answer each question on a separate piece of paper. Be sure to explain your answers.

1. What would a **venerable** person say to you? Why?

2. What kind of problems would a **hermit** have? Explain?

3. What would you want to be **renowned** for? Explain.

4. What would happen if you acted **indifferently** to a friend who was angry with you?

5. What is **essential** to a living thing? Why?

6. Which type of questions do you **ponder** the most? Explain.

7. When might you choose to talk to your best friend **surreptitiously**? Explain.

8. Could you get **accustomed** to taking a nap every day? Explain.

9. What might a **cantankerous** man say if he was given flowers? Why?

10. How would you try to **placate** a baby?

venerable Venerable people deserve respect because they are old and wise.

hermit A hermit is someone who lives alone, far away from other people.

renowned People who are renowned are famous for their skill or talent.

indifferent If you are indifferent to something, you are not for or against it.

essential Something that is essential is absolutely necessary.

ponder If you ponder something, you think about it carefully.

surreptitious Someone who is surreptitious is secretive and sneaky.

accustomed If you are accustomed to something, you are so used to it that it seems normal and comfortable.

cantankerous A cantankerous person complains or argues about everything.

placate If you placate someone, you make that person less angry by doing something to please him or her.

Take It Further

Complete these sentences on a separate piece of paper.

1. The **venerable** judge decided to . . .

2. Mrs. Lincoln became a **hermit** after she . . .

3. The stuntman was **renowned** because he . . .

4. The substitute seemed **indifferent** about his students leaving the classroom, so . . .

5. A good chef knows it is **essential** to . . .

6. Elena likes to take long walks on the trail and **ponder** . . .

7. If you want to give someone a present in a **surreptitious** way, you should . . .

8. Before Caroline got **accustomed** to her new school, she . . .

9. Because the school custodian was in a **cantankerous** mood, he . . .

10. After spilling juice on her dad's tie, Ariella tried to **placate** him by . . .

Explore It

Many words in the English language sound similar to other words with very different meanings. For example, you know that the word *renowned* means "someone who is famous for his or her skill or talent," but are you familiar with the word *renounced*? *Renounced* sounds similar to *renowned*, but means "to officially give up a title or position."

Read the pairs of similar-sounding words and their definitions below. With a partner, write a sentence for each pair of words. Remember that the sentences should clearly show the meaning of each word. Then read your sentences to the class, but leave blank spaces where the words belong. Challenge your classmates to fill in the blanks!

1. allude = to mention something briefly
   elude = to avoid

2. emigrate = to leave a place and live elsewhere
   immigrate = to enter a new country

3. raise = to build up
   raze = to destroy

Example: *The renowned pop star renounced her title as world's best singer after she was caught lip-syncing.*

Unbelievable
Music
Machines

People love music. But for some people, normal musical instruments just won't do. Here are a few of the weirdest and most amazing musical instruments in the world.

Don't Touch The Wires!

The next time you're watching a movie about a mad scientist surreptitiously building a robot in his dark underground laboratory, listen for the spooky sounds of the Theremin. A Russian scientist named Leon Theremin invented the instrument in 1919 when he noticed how the sound of a radio changed as his hands got closer to its antennae. His instrument uses two antennas: one controls the pitch of the sound, or how high or low the note is, and the other antenna controls the volume. The Theremin is a very difficult instrument to get accustomed to because it actually turns off when it is touched. Even though it is used as a serious instrument, the Theremin's unique sound is best known for making creepy background music for science-fiction movies.

Wind Talkers

It takes years to learn how to play some instruments. People lock themselves in their houses like hermits and practice for hours to get it right. But some instruments don't need a musician at all! The Aeolian harp is a small wooden box similar to a guitar, but this guitar plays itself! The ancient Greeks invented the Aeolian harp over 2,000 years ago when they noticed how strings of yarn made humming sounds on top of windy mountains near the ocean. One day a venerable Greek inventor decided to put a string-covered box on one of these mountains, and it started to make beautiful music. The Greeks named the new instrument after Aeolus, the god of wind.

Microscopic Rocker

What is the smallest instrument in the world? If you said the harmonica, your guess is about 100,000 times too large. The nanoguitar was created in 1997 by scientists working at New York's renowned Cornell University. It is only ten micrometers long—the same size as one of the five million tiny red blood cells floating around in your body. It is so small that it can only be seen using a powerful microscope and can only be played using a microscopic laser!

Rev Up Your Writing

You've read about several unusual musical instruments. Write about a time when you heard or played some interesting music. How did the music make you feel? What did you learn from the experience? Use as many of the vocabulary words as possible but make sense.

51

Word Organizer

Copy this graphic organizer onto a separate piece of paper.

Indifference is in the center of the Word-O-Meter. Think of words that would be hotter or colder than *indifference*. Write your answers in the boxes. Explain your answers.

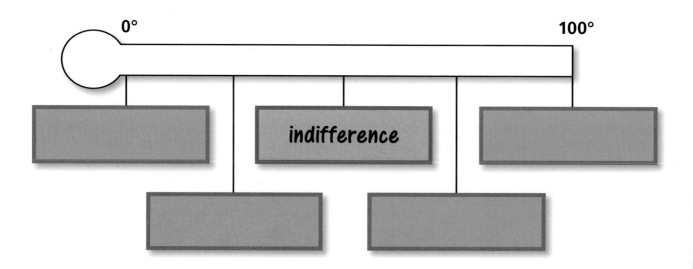

0°   100°

indifference

"There is nothing harder
than the softness of indifference."
—Juan Montalvo

How NOT to Write a Thank You Note

When Greg's mom saw this piece of paper crumpled up near Greg's desk, she was furious. She knew that he had sent Aunt Sylvia the perfect thank you note—she had read it herself—but she had never dreamed that this was the one he had really wanted to send!

Fleur de Lavande

Dear Aunt Sylvia,

My mom said I have to write you a thank you note. She said that I can't play basketball until I do. So, in order to placate her, I'll scribble something down and hope it makes her happy.

You sent me a bottle of lavender soap for my birthday. Now, I'm sure you had a good reason for doing this. I have pondered this for a while and have come up with the following: You think I smell.

You obviously have no idea who I am or what I'm all about. If you did, you would have sent me a skateboard, or maybe a new video game—but you would never have thought that a bottle of soap would be essential to my happiness.

Or maybe, just maybe, you sent it to me because it was the cheapest thing you could possibly find, and you wanted the excitement of getting a thank you note in the mail. If that's true, I hope you enjoyed this one!

Your nephew,

Greg

The Worst Gift EVER!

Last week we asked our readers: What is the worst gift you've ever received? It didn't take long for letters to flood our office. Take notes, so you know what NOT to give as a gift!

My grandma always gives me socks for my birthday, which is in the middle of July. Who needs socks when it's 100 degrees outside? I always pretend that the socks are the greatest things I've ever seen. Maybe that's why she keeps getting them for me. Perhaps if I act indifferent next year, she'll get the hint!

Jermaine, 14

My mother and I share the same birthday. One year, my dad gave my mom and me matching outfits. I had asked for some DVDs and CDs; instead, my dad showed up with frilly, pink dresses. I don't know what made him think that I would want to dress like my mom. That gift put me in a cantankerous mood for the rest of the day. I didn't even want to eat cake! Note to the fathers out there: Don't buy your daughters anything to wear. It's not a good idea!

Caroline, 13

During the holiday season, my aunt and uncle always send me a box of trail mix. Talk about the world's worst snack, let alone gift. You would think that my own aunt and uncle would know that I'm allergic to nuts and that I don't like dried fruit. I wonder if they'll ever get a clue!

Amaya, 12

Rev Up Your Writing

Greg wrote two letters to his aunt Sylvia. You read the rude thank you letter, but what about the one he did send? Write the second, more polite thank you letter. Use as many of the vocabulary words as possible but make sense.

Can You Relate?

Copy this graphic organizer onto a separate piece of paper. Match the following words with their related vocabulary word. If a word relates to more than one vocabulary word, explain why.

bemoan   If you bemoan something, you complain about it.
conspiracy   A conspiracy is a secret plan to do something wrong.
cryptic   Cryptic messages have hidden meanings or are hard to understand.
rancor   Someone who feels rancor feels anger toward something.
speculate   If you speculate about something, you think about all of the possible outcomes.

surreptitious	ponder	cantankerous

In Your Own Words

Respond to one of the following prompts on a separate piece of paper. As you respond, use as many of the vocabulary words as possible. Be creative but make sense!

▶ Write about a time when you or someone you know wanted to be alone. What did you do? Why did you want to be alone?

▶ Write a fable about someone who lives alone in a forest. Make some of the characters animals if you like. Don't forget to teach a moral lesson.

▶ Write about a topic of your choice.

VOCABULARY

venerable
hermit
renowned
indifferent
essential
ponder
surreptitious
accustomed
cantankerous
placate

TRAPPED

By Aron Ralston

In April, 2003, mountain climber Aron Ralston set out on what he thought would be an easy solo climb. Midway through the climb, Ralson was trapped under a half-ton boulder. How far would he go to make it out alive?

By 2:30, I'm about seven miles into the canyon, at the midpoint of my descent, the narrow slot above the 65-foot-high rappel[1] marked as Big Drop in my guidebook. . . .

I reach the first drop-off in the floor of the canyon, a ten-foot dryfall, and use a few good in-cut handholds on the canyon's left wall to lower myself. . . .

The pale sky is still visible above this ten-foot-wide gash in the earth's surface as I continue scrambling down, over lips and ledges and under chockstones—boulders suspended between the canyon walls. The canyon narrows to just four feet wide here, undulating and twisting and deepening. It's 2:41 P.M. . . .

Right in front of me, just below the ledge, is a second chockstone the size of a large bus tire, stuck fast in the three-foot channel between the walls. If I can step onto it, I can dangle off the chockstone, then take a short fall to the canyon floor. . . . With a few precautionary jabs, I kick down at the boulder. It's jammed tightly enough that it will hold my weight. I lower myself from the chimneying position[2] and step onto the chockstone. It supports me but teeters slightly. . . .

. . . Instantly, I know this is trouble, and instinctively I let go of the rotating boulder to land on the round rocks on the canyon floor. I look up, and the backlit chockstone consumes the sky.[3] Fear shoots my hands over my head. . . .

The next three seconds play out in slow motion. The falling rock smashes my left hand against the south wall; I yank my left arm back as the rock ricochets in the confined space; the boulder then crushes my right hand, thumb up, fingers extended; the rock slides another foot down the wall with my arm in tow, tearing the skin off the lateral[4] side of my forearm. Then, silence. . . .

3 P.M.

. . . The flaring agony throws me into a panic. I grimace and growl. . . . I yank my arm three times in a naive attempt to pull it out from under the rock. But I'm stuck.

. . . I shove against the boulder, heaving against it, pushing with my left hand, lifting with my knees pressed under the rock. I brace my thighs under the boulder and thrust upward, grunting, "Come on . . . move!"

Nothing. . . .

FOOTNOTES

[1] *rappel:* the descent of a cliff wall
[2] *chimneying position:* bracing one's feet against opposite walls
[3] *consumes the sky:* fills his view of the sky
[4] *lateral:* the side farthest from the body

"OK," I say out loud, "time to relax. The adrenaline's not going to get you out of here. Let's look this over, see what we got." I need to start thinking; to do that, I need to be calm. Poking my left hand into the small gap above the catch point,[5] I touch my right thumb, which is already a sickly gray. It's cocked sideways and looks terribly unnatural. There is no feeling in my right hand at all. . . .

. . . I organize my options in order of preference: excavate the rock around my hand with my multitool knife; rig ropes and an anchor above myself to lift the boulder off my hand; or amputate my arm.

I decide to work on the first option—chipping the rock away. Drawing out my multitool, I unfold the longer of the two blades.

My first attempt to saw into the boulder barely scuffs the rock. I try again, pressing harder, but the back of the knife handle indents my forefinger much more readily than the cutting edge scores[6] the rock. . . .

8 P.M.

Stress turns into pessimism. Without enough water to wait for rescue, without a pick to crack the boulder, without a rigging system to lift it, I have one course of action. I speak slowly out loud:

"You're gonna have to cut your arm off."

Hearing the words makes my instincts and emotions revolt. My vocal cords tense and my voice changes octaves:

"But I don't wanna cut my arm off!"

"Aron, you're gonna have to cut your arm off."

I realize I'm arguing with myself, and yield to a halfhearted chuckle. This is crazy. But I know that I could never saw through my arm bones with either of the blades of my multitool. . . .

DAY TWO: SUNDAY, APRIL 27
2 P.M.

For the first time, I seriously contemplate amputating my arm. . . . My two biggest concerns are a cutting tool that can do the job and a tourniquet that will keep me from bleeding out. Of the multitool's blades, the inch-and-a-half one is sharper than the three-inch one. It will be important to use only the longer blade for hacking at the chockstone and preserve the shorter one for potential surgery.

FOOTNOTES

[5] *catch point:* the place where the climber's hand is caught

[6] *scores:* makes a cut into

Even with the sharper blade, I instinctually understand that I won't be able to hack through my bones—I don't have anything that could approximate even a rudimentary saw. . . .

. . . Until I figure out how to cut through the bones, amputation isn't a practical choice. But I wonder about my courage levels if cutting off my arm becomes a real plan of action. As a test, I hold the shorter blade of the multitool to my skin. The tip pokes between the tendons and veins a few inches up from my trapped wrist, indenting my flesh. The sight repulses me. . . .

I can't do it. . .

DAY THREE: MONDAY, APRIL 28
7 A.M.

. . . I take my multitool and, without thinking, open the long blade. Instead of pointing the tip into the tendon gap at my wrist, I hold it with the blade against the upper part of my forearm. Surprising myself, I press on the blade and slowly draw the knife across my forearm. Nothing happens. Huh. I press harder. Still nothing. No cut, no blood, nothing. Back and forth, I vigorously saw at my arm, growing more frustrated with each attempt. Exasperated, I give up. . .

DAY FOUR: TUESDAY, APRIL 29
7:58 A.M.

Slowly, I become aware of the cold stare of my knife. There's a reason for everything, including why I brought that knife, and suddenly I know what I am about to do. . . . .

Unfolding the shorter blade, I close the handle and grasp it in my fist. Raising the tool above my right arm, I pick a spot on the top of my forearm. I hesitate, jerking my left hand to a halt a foot above my target. Then I recock my tool and, before I can stop myself, my fist violently thrusts the blade down, burying it to the hilt[7] in the meat of my forearm. . . .

My vision warps with astonishment. . . . When I grasp the tool more firmly and wiggle it slightly, the blade connects with something hard, my upper forearm bone. . . .

. . . Even damped by surrounding tissues, the hollow thumping of the blade against my upper forearm bone resonates[8] up into my elbow. The soft *thock-thock-thock* tells me I have reached the end of this experiment. I cannot cut into or through my forearm bones. . . .

FOOTNOTES
[7] *to the hilt:* completely
[8] *resonates:* makes a loud vibration

DAY FIVE: WEDNESDAY, APRIL 30
2 P.M.

. . . Somewhere inside my mind, I know I won't survive tonight in Blue John Canyon. The day has been cool; this night will be the worst yet. . . .

DAY SIX: THURSDAY, MAY 1
9:30 A.M.

. . . I can't hold my head upright; it lolls off to lean against the canyon wall. I am a zombie. I am the undead. . . .

I thrash myself forward and back, side to side, up and down, down and up. I scream out in pure hate, shrieking as I batter my body against the canyon walls, losing every bit of composure that I've struggled so intensely to maintain. And then I feel my arm bend unnaturally in the unbudging grip of the chockstone. An epiphany strikes me. . . .

There is no hesitation. . . . I put my left hand under the boulder and push hard, harder, HARDER! to put a maximum downward force on my radius bone. As I slowly bend my arm down to the left, a POW! reverberates like a muted cap-gun shot. . . .

. . . Without further pause and again in silence . . . I push with my legs, . . . pulling with every bit of ferocity I can muster, until a second cap-gun shot ends my ulna's[9] anticipation. Sweating and euphoric, I touch my right arm again. Both bones have splintered in the same place, just above my wrist. . . .

In a blaze of pain, I know the job is just starting.

FOOTNOTES

....

[9] *ulna:* the long, thin bone in the forearm

Explain Yourself

Answer each question on a separate piece of paper. Be sure to explain your answers.

1. Do you think a cheerleader would be **pessimistic**? Why or why not?

2. What games do you have a **rudimentary** knowledge of? Explain.

3. If your father cooked a dinner that **repulsed** you, would you eat it? Why or why not?

4. How confident would you feel if you studied **vigorously** for a test? Explain.

5. Would you want to be friends with someone who **exasperates** you? Why or why not?

6. If you had an **epiphany** during a math quiz, would you get a good grade? Explain.

7. Would a whisper be likely to **reverberate**? Why or why not?

8. What news could make you feel **euphoric**? Why?

9. What kind of school project would you **agonize** over? Explain.

10. Name something that you would do **methodically**. Explain.

VOCABULARY

pessimism   Pessimism is when you expect the worst or see only the negative side of things.

rudimentary   Something that is rudimentary is very simple and not completely developed.

repulse   If something repulses you, it disgusts you so much that you want to get away from it.

vigorously   When you do something vigorously, you do it with lots of energy.

exasperate   If someone or something exasperates you, it makes you very angry or frustrated.

epiphany   When you have an epiphany, you suddenly understand something clearly or have a great idea.

reverberate   If a loud sound reverberates, it echoes around you and seems to shake the place you are in.

euphoric   When you are euphoric, you are extremely happy.

agonize   If you agonize about something, you worry about it for a long time.

methodical   Someone who is methodical does things very carefully and step by step.

Take It Further

Complete these sentences on a separate piece of paper.

1. Debbie's **pessimism** grew when she . . .

2. It was clear that Than's knowledge of math was **rudimentary** because . . .

3. When she saw her new room, Katarina was **repulsed** by . . .

4. Terrence played **vigorously** at first, but in the last few minutes of the game he . . .

5. My brother's excuses **exasperated** me so much that I . . .

6. Mei had an **epiphany** during the movie when . . .

7. Everyone in the building still felt the **reverberations** from . . .

8. This morning, Darnell was **euphoric** because . . .

9. I **agonized** over the thought of talking to Michael because . . .

10. Alejandro was very **methodical** when he . . .

Explore It

One word can take many different forms. For example:

Vigorously is an adverb that means "with lots of energy."
Vigorous is an adjective that means "energetic."
Vigor is a noun that means "high energy."

With a partner, write a poem using the words *vigor, vigorous,* and *vigorously.*
Try to rhyme the words with other words in your poem. For example, you
might begin your poem by saying:

> I always exercise with vigor.
> That's why my muscles are getting bigger!

Can you find words that rhyme with *vigor, vigorous,* and *vigorously?* If not,
be creative and make up a new word!

Scandal on the Stage

LOS ANGELES—Anger and confusion rocked the stage last night when popular singer "Warbling" Will Casper was caught lip-syncing during a concert.

Casper, the lead singer of the band Slime Mold, ran into trouble about halfway through the concert. As the band played its hit song, "Everyone Buy Our CD," Casper got distracted by a fan who was dancing offbeat. Suddenly, Casper's singing could be heard through the loudspeakers, even though his mouth was not moving.

Fans were outraged and began to boo and throw things at the stage. The band was forced to flee the building through a back exit, ending the concert. "I'm just repulsed by this," said one concertgoer. "Warbling Will is a fake! He doesn't sing his songs live!"

"Will lip-syncs all the time," said the band's drummer, Biff Foyle. "We thought everyone knew that."

Adding to Casper's troubles is the fact that the voice Casper was lip-syncing to wasn't even his own. "No, that's definitely not him," said Diana Casper, Casper's mother.

"OK, look," said an exasperated Casper. "I don't actually do any singing. I hire someone else to do it. But that's only because I have a terrible singing voice! What's the problem? Why is there so much pessimism?"

Casper added, "I'm sure our fans will stay with us, no matter what."

What a Show!

To | Nadia Truman

 Attach   Address   Fonts

SEND

Subject | What a Show!

Nadia,
I know you're bummed because you couldn't come to the Slime Mold concert, but I have to tell you something that you won't believe! Mrs. Holmes was at the concert! Yes, our shy, quiet librarian was crowd-surfing in the first row! She had on leather pants and a sparkly shirt. I had to rub my eyes to make sure I was seeing clearly. It was insane! I moved as far as possible from that part of the crowd so she wouldn't notice me.

Anyway . . . the band rocked! They pulled out the laser lights and all that other good stuff. And I can't even describe to you how loud they were. The guitars are still reverberating in my ears.

By the way, they saved our favorite song for last. I thought they weren't going to play it, so I was euphoric when they did! I sang twice as loud as usual—in your honor! :)

Needless to say, Mrs. Holmes and I had a blast. ;)
Next time, please try not to be grounded.
Sorry for rubbing it in. :)
See you tomorrow.
—Dana

> **Pessimism,** when you get used to it, is just as agreeable as **optimism.**
> —*Arnold Bennett*

Rev Up Your Writing

Have you ever been to a live musical performance? Write about your experience. If you have never been to one, write about the kinds of music that you enjoy. Use as many of the vocabulary words as possible but make sense.

Word Organizer

Copy this graphic organizer onto a separate piece of paper.

List events that might make you euphoric in the top half of the Word Wheel.
List events that would not make you euphoric in the bottom half.

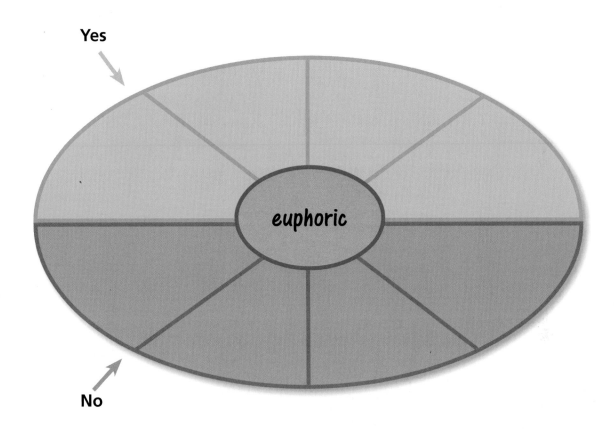

Yes

euphoric

No

The Screenplay That Wrote Itself

[Fade in. A teenage boy, DEREK, is sitting at a desk in the middle of the room. He is writing on a piece of paper. He stops quickly and angrily crumples up the paper. Enter SOPHIE, Derek's older sister.]

SOPHIE: You've been agonizing over that project for hours, Derek. Have you made any progress?

DEREK: Nope. I tried to write about a detective solving a mystery, but I just started and it's pretty rudimentary. Then I wrote about people stuck on a desert island. Then I tried astronauts in space, but nothing seems to work.

SOPHIE: Maybe you could combine all of those somehow.

DEREK: What, a detective stuck on a desert island in space? That's ridiculous, Sophie. I wish this screenplay would just write itself. Wait...that's it! I just had an epiphany! I'm going to write a screenplay about writing a screenplay!

SOPHIE: What? What do you mean?

DEREK: I'll write about what's happening right now. You and I will be the characters. The screenplay will be about me, writing a screenplay. I'll just methodically write down everything you and I have said so far.

[Derek takes out another piece of paper and starts to write vigorously for a few minutes.]

DEREK: I'm finished. Do you want to read it, Sophie?

[Sophie tries to speak, but nothing comes out. She points to the page Derek has been writing on.]

DEREK: You mean that you can only speak if I write a line for you! [He laughs wickedly.] Oh, I'm going to have fun with this!

[Fade out.]

Rev Up Your Writing

Think of a time when you had an epiphany. Was it an idea for a story or a project? Was it a solution to an everyday problem? Write about your idea and how you came up with it. Use as many of the vocabulary words as possible but make sense.

67

Can You Relate?

Copy this graphic organizer onto a separate piece of paper. Match the following words with their related vocabulary word. If a word relates to more than one vocabulary word, explain why.

deprecate   When you deprecate something, you criticize or denounce it.
malcontent   A malcontent is someone who is not happy.
morose   When you are morose, you are gloomy or bad tempered.
odious   When something is odious, it is hateful.
offensive   When something is offensive, it is insulting or disgusting.

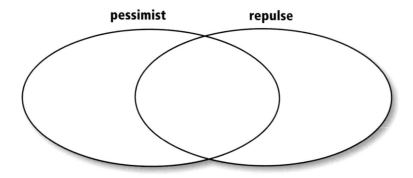

In Your Own Words

Respond to one of the following prompts on a separate piece of paper. As you respond, use as many of the vocabulary words as possible. Be creative but make sense!

▶ Describe a time when you or someone you know was close to achieving a goal but failed. What did you learn as a result? What might you do differently next time?

▶ Write a review describing your favorite movie or TV show. Describe the characters and summarize the plot. Then explain why people should see it.

▶ Write about a topic of your choice.

VOCABULARY

pessimism
rudimentary
repulse
vigorously
exasperate
epiphany
reverberate
euphoric
agonize
methodical

from SOJOURNER TRUTH

Ain't I a Woman?

By Patricia and Fredrick McKissack

At an 1851 gathering about women's rights, Sojourner Truth, a freed slave, dared to challenge the crowd. Would she be allowed to speak? Would anyone listen?

The gathering was large but for the most part congenial. Suddenly, the doors swung open and a tall, proud figure stood framed in the doorway. "It's Sojourner Truth," someone whispered. Slowly Sojourner walked to the front of the church, noticing she was the only black person there. Since there were no seats left, she took a seat on the steps to the pulpit. She folded her arms and listened.

Soon the room was buzzing.[1] Was a black woman going to speak?

One speaker after another came to the podium, each trying to impress his or her opinion upon the crowd. Several preachers tried to disrupt the meeting by encouraging women . . . to leave immediately. When that didn't work, the preachers used the same tired logic that had been used for centuries to oppress women and blacks: *God created women to be weak and blacks to be a subservient race. . . .*

Another man quoted a newspaper article which suggested that "a woman's place is at home taking care of her children. *(What?* thought Sojourner. *Nobody ever gave me that opportunity.). . .*

During a brief intermission, a group of women cornered Frances Gage[2] and questioned whether Sojourner would be allowed to speak. They were afraid that having a black woman speak might confuse the issues and even discredit their cause. After all, *what has women's rights to do with abolition?*[3] Some of the "leading" ladies were threatening to leave.

"Let's just see," Mrs. Gage answered, making no commitment either way.

When the next session began, Sojourner approached the pulpit. "No, no, don't let her speak," several men and women called out.

Sojourner turned to the chairwoman asking for permission. Gage hesitated momentarily, then simply introduced her, "Sojourner Truth." That's all that was needed.

By then Sojourner was used to facing hostile crowds. Fearlessly, but gently, she took control of the situation. First, she removed her sunbonnet, folded it neatly and set it aside. Her slow deliberate movements had a calming effect on the audience. . . .

With no prepared speech in front of her she began in a deep, husky voice:

FOOTNOTES

[1] *buzzing:* lively; full of noise
[2] *Frances Gage:* the organizer of the gathering
[3] *abolition:* the movement to end slavery

"Well, Children, where there is so much racket,[4] there must be somethin' out of kilter[5]. . . . The white men will be in a fix pretty soon. But what's all this about anyway?

"That man over there," she said pointing to a minister who had said a woman's place was to be mother, wife and companion, good sister, and loving niece. Among other things he also said women were the "weaker sex."

To this Sojourner took issue.[6] "He says women need to be helped into carriages and lifted over ditches and to have the best everywhere. Nobody ever helps me into carriages, over mud puddles, or gets me any best places."

And raising herself to her full height, she asked, "And ain't I a woman?"

Sojourner turned to the men who were seated behind her. "Look at me!" She bared her right arm and raised it in the air. The audience gasped as one voice. Her dark arm was muscular, made strong by hard work. "I have ploughed. And I have planted." No doubt she was remembering the year she had worked for Dumont to earn early freedom. "And I have gathered into barns. And no man could head me." She paused again and asked this time in a whisper. "And ain't I a woman?"

"I have borne . . . children and seen them sold into slavery, and when I cried out in a mother's grief, none heard me but Jesus. And ain't I a woman?". . .

She challenged the widely held belief that women were less intelligent than men, and blacks had no intellect at all. . . . Her common sense ripped at the core of[7] [the people's] hypocrisy.

. . . Few listeners at the time could understand the full import[8] of what Sojourner Truth was really saying in that hard-hitting "Ain't I a Woman" speech. It is doubtful the rural community was ready to accept the claim that took women's rights across the boundaries of race, class, and the bondage of slavery.

Sojourner's "truth" was simple. Racism and sexism were unacceptable to people of good reason.

FOOTNOTES
4 *racket:* noise
5 *out of kilter:* wrong
6 *took issue:* disagreed
7 *ripped at the core of:* showed the basic wrongness of
8 *import:* importance

Explain Yourself

Answer each question on a separate piece of paper. Be sure to explain your answers.

1. Would you be angry if somebody called you **congenial**? Explain.

2. Have you ever felt **oppressed**? Explain.

3. Would you want your friend to feel **subservient** to you? Why or why not?

4. Is it ever right to **discredit** someone? Explain.

5. If you saw a **hostile** person at your front door, what would you do?

6. Is it possible to **deliberately** make a mistake? Explain.

7. Have you ever been guilty of **hypocrisy**? Explain.

8. Do you think friends should **chastise** each other? Why or why not?

9. Would you **advocate** going to a concert the night before a big test? Why or why not?

10. What might you **galvanize** the people in your neighborhood to do? Explain.

congenial   People who are congenial are friendly and easy to get along with.

oppress   When you oppress people, you take away their freedom to make their own decisions.

subservient   If you are subservient, you do whatever someone else wants you to do.

discredit   When you discredit people, you hurt their reputation by pointing out what they have done wrong.

hostile   Someone who is hostile is angry and may act in a mean or dangerous way.

deliberate   A deliberate action is one that is done on purpose, often slowly and with care.

hypocrisy   Hypocrisy is saying you believe something but acting in a different way.

chastise   When you chastise people, you scold them for their misbehavior.

advocate   When you are an advocate of something, you publicly support it and believe in it.

galvanize   If you galvanize a group of people, you motivate or inspire them to act.

Take It Further

Complete these sentences on a separate piece of paper.

1. Esther is more **congenial** than David because . . .

2. Mateo felt that his older brother was **oppressing** him when . . .

3. I am **subservient** to my mother because . . .

4. The presidential candidate **discredited** her opponent by saying . . .

5. Megan's **hostility** was clear when she suddenly . . .

6. "You did that **deliberately**!" Enrico said after Ann . . .

7. Tabitha thought her older brother was a **hypocrite** because he . . .

8. Juan **chastised** his little brother for . . .

9. After hearing the speech, Ashley became an **advocate** of . . .

10. The coach tried to **galvanize** the soccer team by . . .

Explore It

You may know what homonyms are (words that are pronounced the same but mean different things, like *to, too,* and *two*), but did you know there are also heteronyms? Heteronyms are words that are spelled the same but pronounced differently in different contexts. One example of this is *close* (as in nearby) and *close* (as in "close the door"). Another example is your vocabulary word *advocate*.

Listen to the sentences your teacher reads and identify whether the sentence is using *advocate* as a noun or a verb. Then, working in pairs or small groups, take one of the following words and write sentences for it that demonstrate the different meanings and pronunciations of the word. Be ready to present to the class!

address	buffet	content	desert	dove
minute	object	present	read	rebel
record	resume	separate	tear	wind

Profile of a SUPERTEAM

In a hostile world where villains oppress all free people and seek to discredit anyone good and noble, a team of heroes has risen to battle evil and hypocrisy and become advocates for all humankind.

Mr. Mephitis

Superpower: The Stink Bomb can release a stench worse than 1,000 skunks mixed with 1,000 rotten eggs.

Interests/hobbies: gardening, mud baths, and defeating super villains

Greatest Superhero moment: In the spring riots of 2054, the Stink Bomb turned back a hostile mob by stinking up five square miles of city property.

Biggest Superpower challenge: smelling good enough to go on a date

Quote: "Crime stinks, but so do I!"

a.k.a.
The Stink
Bomb

Mrs. Adjusto

Superpower: Lady Stretch can adjust the width of her body from the thickness of a sheet of paper to the thickness of a city block.

Interests/hobbies: eating contests, wind surfing, and saving humankind from oppression

Greatest Superhero moment: When enemies invaded her city, Lady Stretch blocked the entire street and prevented troops from moving past her.

Biggest Superpower challenge: dealing with her stretch marks during bathing suit season

Quote: "There's no threat too thick or too thin for me to handle."

a.k.a
Lady Stretch

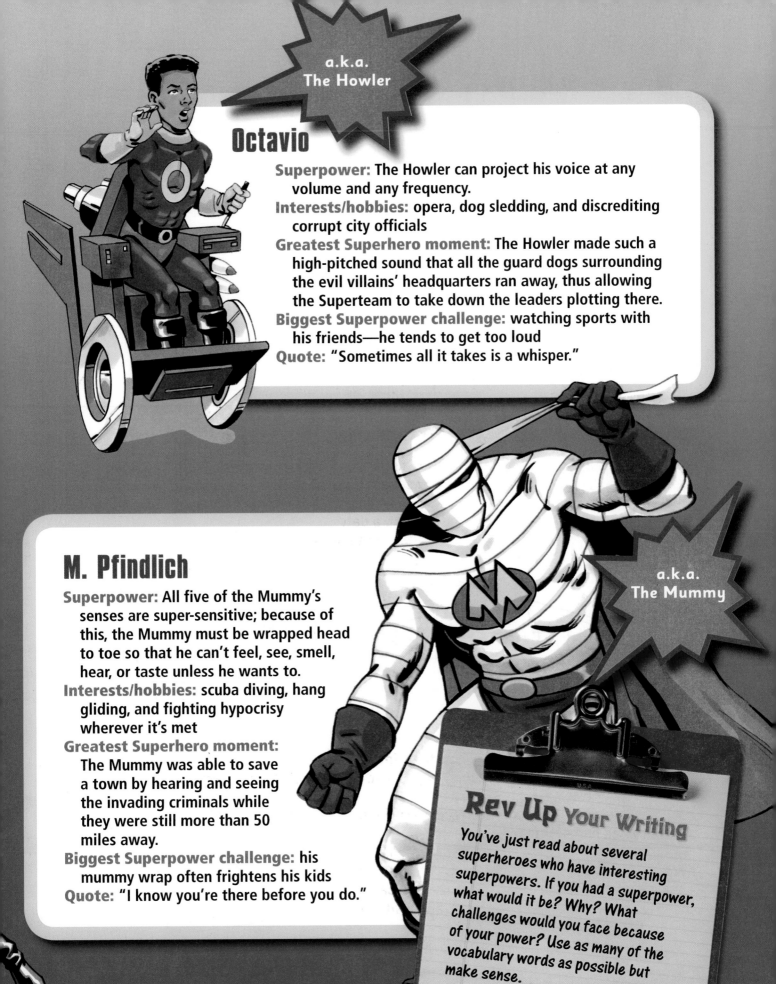

a.k.a. The Howler

Octavio

Superpower: The Howler can project his voice at any volume and any frequency.

Interests/hobbies: opera, dog sledding, and discrediting corrupt city officials

Greatest Superhero moment: The Howler made such a high-pitched sound that all the guard dogs surrounding the evil villains' headquarters ran away, thus allowing the Superteam to take down the leaders plotting there.

Biggest Superpower challenge: watching sports with his friends—he tends to get too loud

Quote: "Sometimes all it takes is a whisper."

M. Pfindlich

Superpower: All five of the Mummy's senses are super-sensitive; because of this, the Mummy must be wrapped head to toe so that he can't feel, see, smell, hear, or taste unless he wants to.

Interests/hobbies: scuba diving, hang gliding, and fighting hypocrisy wherever it's met

Greatest Superhero moment: The Mummy was able to save a town by hearing and seeing the invading criminals while they were still more than 50 miles away.

Biggest Superpower challenge: his mummy wrap often frightens his kids

Quote: "I know you're there before you do."

a.k.a. The Mummy

Rev Up Your Writing

You've just read about several superheroes who have interesting superpowers. If you had a superpower, what would it be? Why? What challenges would you face because of your power? Use as many of the vocabulary words as possible but make sense.

75

SSON 6

DAY
6

Word Organizer

Copy this graphic organizer onto a separate piece of paper.

List words that are synonyms of *congenial*. Write your answers in the Synonyms box. Use some of the words in this box to describe a celebrity who you think is congenial.

Then list words that are antonyms of *congenial*. Write your answers in the Antonyms box. Use some of the words in this box to describe a celebrity who you think is not congenial.

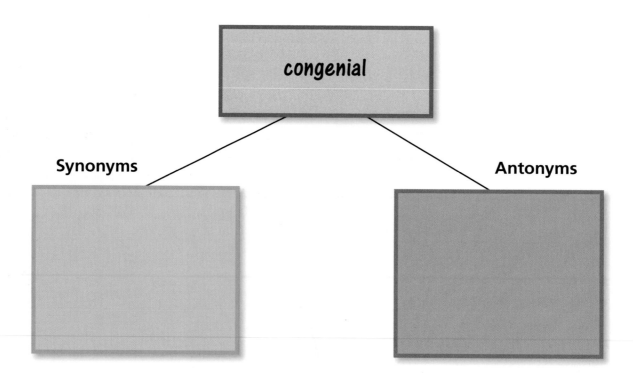

Synonyms

Antonyms

congenial

Locked In!

SPLAT!

I was hit.

I looked down at the spitball that was stuck to the sleeve of my favorite sweater.

"Wonderful," I muttered as I removed the saliva-infested wad.

Why had I ever agreed to chaperone the lock-in for a bunch of middle school kids? Sure, I got credit for doing community service. But what sane high school student would purposely put herself in the middle of this chaos?

It's not like I expected my group to be subservient, but I did think that they would listen to me. Instead, my group of ten students was the wildest, rowdiest bunch. All the other chaperones had control of their groups, and they looked at me like I was as bad as my out-of-control kids.

So what if my group had gotten into the library and rearranged all the books and then pulled the toilet paper out of the bathroom and down the hall in one long streamer? I was tired of the nasty looks from the other chaperones. I decided that I needed to galvanize my group into following the rules. I begged them to behave. I even tried to bribe them with candy. And I think it worked! They have huddled together and are talking quietly to each other and occasionally looking over at me.

I mean, how much trouble can they get into just talking, right? Right? Uh oh . . .

from
Memoirs of a Dog Walker

By Kate Thorn

My first summer as a dog walker started like any other—hot. Our local pool had begun charging $1 for admission. Seeing as how I wouldn't have lasted one week without the sweet relief of swimming, I knew that I needed to get a summer job to start earning some cash. My parents suggested I start walking Dr. Lu's dog for her during the day while she was working. My first couple of walks were flawless. Snowpea, Dr. Lu's tiny white terrier, was a congenial, obedient dog, and I started to think about how easy it would be to earn more money if I walked multiple dogs. I put up flyers around my neighborhood, and within a week I had more than ten clients! That's when the chaos began.

Walking one small terrier is nothing compared to walking seven or eight bigger dogs, all at the same time! The dogs would run and bark and get their leashes all tangled up playing with each other. I tried chastising and scolding them, but nothing seemed to work. Half of them would pull me to the left while the other half pulled me to the right; it almost seemed like they were doing it deliberately! By the time I got home from my walks, I was so sore and exhausted that I never had the energy to go swim! I finished my first summer as a dog walker a little wealthier and a lot stronger than I started it; my life as a dog walker had begun!

Rev Up Your Writing

In both of these selections, the narrator is trying to handle an out-of-control situation. Write about a time when you took control of a situation. Use as many of the vocabulary words as possible but make sense.

Can You Relate?

Copy this graphic organizer onto a separate piece of paper. Match the following words with their related vocabulary word. If a word relates to more than one vocabulary word, explain why.

comply If you comply, you agree to do what somebody tells you to do.
denigrate Someone who denigrates you ruins your reputation.
envenom Something that envenoms you causes you to feel bitter and upset.
stimulate Someone who stimulates other people motivates them to take action.
subordinate If you are subordinate to others, you have a lower position than they do.

subservient	discredit	galvanize

In Your Own Words

Respond to one of the following prompts on a separate piece of paper. As you respond, use as many of the vocabulary words as possible. Be creative but make sense!

▶ Write about a time when you or someone you know was in charge of another person or thing. Explain any difficulty encountered and tell how the trouble was resolved.

▶ Write a persuasive article in which you argue what the best superhero power would be. Be sure to tell why it would be better than all the others!

▶ Write about a topic of your choice.

VOCABULARY

congenial
oppress
subservient
discredit
hostile
deliberate
hypocrisy
chastise
advocate
galvanize

DARKNESS
at Noon

By Harold Krents
Illustrated by Denny Bond

What would life be like if you were blind? How would others treat you? The author takes you along on his journey through life and describes various encounters with people and their reactions to his disability.

Blind from birth, I have never had the opportunity to see myself and have been completely dependent on the image I create in the eye of the observer. To date it has not been narcissistic.

There are those who assume that since I can't see, I obviously also cannot hear. Very often people will converse with me at the top of their lungs,[1] enunciating each word very carefully. Conversely, people will also often whisper, assuming that since my eyes don't work, my ears don't either.

For example, when I go to the airport and ask the ticket agent for assistance to the plane, he or she will invariably pick up the phone, call a ground hostess, and whisper: "Hi, Jane, we've got a 76 here." I have concluded that the word blind is not used, for one of two reasons: Either they fear that if the dread word is spoken, the ticket agent's retina will immediately detach, or they are reluctant to inform me of my condition, of which I may not have been previously aware.

On the other hand,[2] others know that of course I can hear, but believe that I can't talk. Often, therefore, when my wife and I go out to dinner, a waiter or waitress will ask Kit if "he would like a drink" to which I respond that "indeed he would."

This point was graphically driven home[3] to me while we were in England. I had been given a year's leave of absence from my Washington law firm to study for a diploma in law at Oxford University. During the year I became ill and was hospitalized. Immediately after admission, I was wheeled down to the X-ray room. Just at the door sat an elderly woman—elderly I would judge from the sound of her voice. "What is his name?" the woman asked the orderly who had been wheeling me.

"What's your name?" the orderly repeated to me.

"Harold Krents," I replied.

"Harold Krents," he repeated.

"When was he born?"

"When were you born?"

"November 5, 1944," I responded.

"November 5, 1944," the orderly intoned.

FOOTNOTES
. . . .
[1] *at the top of their lungs:* very loudly
[2] *on the other hand:* from another point of view
[3] *driven home:* made clear

This procedure continued for approximately five minutes, at which point even my saintlike disposition deserted me. "Look," I finally blurted out, "this is absolutely ridiculous. Okay, granted I can't see, but it's got to have become pretty clear to both of you that I don't need an interpreter."

"He says he doesn't need an interpreter," the orderly reported to the woman.

The toughest misconception of all is the view that because I can't see, I can't work. I was turned down by over forty law firms because of my blindness, even though my qualifications included a cum laude[4] degree from Harvard College and a good ranking in my Harvard Law School class.

The attempt to find employment, the continuous frustration of being told that it was impossible for a blind person to practice law, the rejection letters, based not on my lack of ability but rather on my disability, will always remain one of the most disillusioning[5] experiences of my life.

Fortunately, this view of limitation and exclusion is beginning to change. On April 16, [1978,] the Department of Labor issued regulations that mandate[6] equal-employment opportunities for the handicapped. By and large, the business community's response to offering employment to the disabled has been enthusiastic.

I therefore look forward to the day, with the expectation that it is certain to come, when employers will view their handicapped workers as a little child did me years ago when my family still lived in Scarsdale.

I was playing basketball with my father in our back yard according to procedures we had developed. My father would stand beneath the hoop, shout, and I would shoot over his head at the basket attached to our garage. Our next-door neighbor, aged five, wandered over into our yard with a playmate. "He's blind," our neighbor whispered to her friend in a voice that could be heard distinctly by Dad and me.

FOOTNOTES
. . . .
[4] *cum laude:* Latin for "with praise"
[5] *disillusioning:* disappointing
[6] *mandate:* require

Dad shot and missed; I did the same. Dad hit the rim; I missed entirely; Dad shot and missed the garage entirely. "Which one is blind?" whispered back the little friend.

I would hope that in the near future, when a plant manager is touring the factory with the foreman and comes upon a handicapped and a nonhandicapped person working together, his comment after watching them work will be, "Which one is disabled?"

Explain Yourself

Answer each question on a separate piece of paper. Be sure to explain your answers.

1. If you thought someone was **narcissistic**, would you tell him or her? Explain.

2. Should you **enunciate** your words when you speak in public? Why or why not?

3. What is something you do **invariably**? Explain.

4. Could you easily describe a **graphic** image? Why or why not?

5. Would you enjoy listening to someone **intone** your favorite song? Explain.

6. What kind of **disposition** do you have? Explain.

7. If you **excluded** details from a story you were writing, would it be as interesting? Why or why not?

8. If you were to dress **distinctly**, what would you wear? Explain.

9. What kind of **adversity** might a teenager experience? Explain.

10. What could your friend do to make you **bristle**? Explain.

narcissistic People who are narcissistic think mostly about themselves and admire themselves greatly.

enunciate If you enunciate a word, you pronounce it very clearly.

invariably When something happens invariably, it always happens when you expect it to.

graphically When people describe something graphically, they use so much detail that you feel like you can see it.

intone If you intone something, you say it slowly and clearly and in a flat, dull voice.

disposition Your disposition is your personality or mood.

exclusion An exclusion is something that has been left out on purpose.

distinct If something is distinct, it is clear or obvious.

adversity Adversity is an extremely difficult experience or situation that is hard to overcome.

bristle If you bristle toward someone or something, you act in an angry or irritated way toward it.

Take It Further

Complete these sentences on a separate piece of paper.

1. We knew Henry was **narcissistic** when he . . .

2. Chan asked Megan to **enunciate** because she . . .

3. **Invariably,** our teacher tells us to . . .

4. The author was very **graphic** when she . . .

5. Luis **intoned** the whole essay, so it was . . .

6. Juan's **disposition** is similar to mine because . . .

7. Teesha's party was **exclusive,** so she . . .

8. Azim's art project is **distinct** because . . .

9. Sarita avoided **adversity** when she decided to . . .

10. My parents **bristled** when I told them . . .

Explore It

Words come from many different places in history. The word *narcissistic* comes from Narcissus, a character in Greek mythology. Narcissus was very attractive, and many young women fell in love with him. But Narcissus was not capable of loving anyone but himself. One day when looking into a pond, Narcissus found his true love—his own reflection. He spent night and day gazing lovingly into the pond. Sadly, Narcissus died of rejection because his reflection turned to ripples of water whenever he reached out to touch it. This explains why people who think very highly of themselves are called narcissists.

Working with a partner, choose one of the other vocabulary words and write your own myth to explain the word. Be prepared to share your myth with the class.

Stars of Adversity

These well-known celebrities did not let their personal challenges get in the way of their dreams.

Whoopi Goldberg

Grammy and Golden Globe winner Whoopi Goldberg is probably best known for her roles in many major motion pictures, like *Ghost* and *Sister Act*. Goldberg has become a successful actress despite having a learning disability. Dyslexia causes people to have difficulty remembering and recognizing letters, words, and numbers. Goldberg can describe in graphic detail what it was like growing up, but she didn't know anything about dyslexia as a child. Goldberg says that people suggested that she was "slow." Goldberg, however, always knew she was intelligent. "We're born with success," she says. "It is only others who point out our failures." Although Goldberg will always have dyslexia, it hasn't stopped her from achieving great success.

Michael J. Fox

Michael J. Fox is probably best known for his role as the lively, smart aleck Marty McFly in the *Back to the Future* movie series. In 2000, he left his hit show *Spin City* because he had been diagnosed with Parkinson's disease. This disease can cause uncontrollable tremors, or shaking, and muffled or indistinct speech, among other things. Although Fox still appears on television shows, he spends much of his time spreading Parkinson's awareness and working to find a cure.

Marlee Matlin

Marlee Matlin is a talented actress who has starred in several feature films and television shows. When Matlin was 18 months old, she suffered from an extremely high fever that caused her to become deaf. An ordinary person might bristle at the idea of becoming deaf, but Matlin embraced it. Matlin claims that, ". . . the greatest handicap of deafness does not lie in the ear, it lies in the mind."

James Earl Jones

James Earl Jones has one of the most distinctive voices in Hollywood. He is best known for his role as the voice of Darth Vader in *Star Wars*. However, few people realize that he struggles with a speech disorder. Dysphemia, or stuttering, causes people to have trouble enunciating their words. Jones stuttered so severely as a child that he rarely spoke to anyone and communicated mostly through writing.

Rev Up Your Writing

You've just read about several stars who have overcome adversity. Write about a time when you faced adversity. How did you feel? How did you overcome it? Use as many of the vocabulary words as possible but make sense.

Word Organizer

Copy this graphic organizer onto a separate piece of paper.

Write an explanation of the word *exclusion* in the Explain It box below. Then write a sentence using the word *exclusion* in the Use It box. Finally, use the Sketch It box to sketch a picture that shows the word *exclusion*. Explain your work.

exclusion **Write It**	**Explain It**
Use It	**Sketch It**

Music for Me

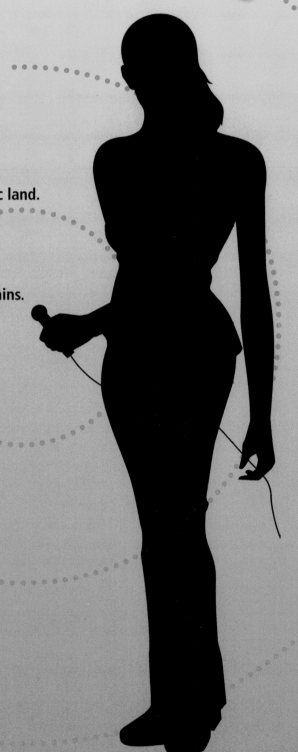

Pain-in-the-brain beat
My ears overheat, feeling wack
Flip, skip that.
Push scan
Hear a cushion of a song, no impact.
All feeling excluded
And my button hand
Sneaks me out of grieve-y, weepy, sleepy music land.
A music lover
Looking for the best of the buffet—
No, get me away
From the strains
Of a bouncy, let's-play world where no one complains.
Even the radio should intone
At least a bit
Of life's invariable confusion.
But these songs
Lead me to the conclusion
Of a false reality.
It means nothing to me
And I can't stand
The empty feelings.
You see
I'm musically
Alone.

Guess I just gotta make my own.

Poetry
An Extreme Sport?

SLAM!

The word is rude, sudden, and "in your face"—a lot like poetry.

If you're a slam poet, that is.

Slam poetry started in Chicago in the mid-1980s. Construction worker Marc Smith, who hosted weekly poetry readings at a jazz club, was looking for an edge. He wanted something fresh and exciting, something that would keep an audience coming back for more.

His solution? Pit poets against each other.

In a typical slam, poets read in rounds. Each poet has three minutes to perform an original work, and judges from the audience decide who makes the next round. The poets who make that special connection with the audience have the best chance to win the finals and earn bragging rights. Those with a nervous disposition will likely be sent packing.

Critics of slam poetry reject this approach to creating poetry. They believe poetry belongs in the classroom. However, a style that started as a gimmick has become a new art form. Today, slam events stretch worldwide, reaching young, enthusiastic audiences.

Much like rap or hip-hop music, slam poetry is about communicating thoughts and emotions in a rhythmic, intense way. All styles are welcome. In fact, it is not uncommon to find slam poets shouting, stomping, and dancing!

Do you like extremes? Are you a narcissist looking for an audience?

Slam poetry might just be the thrill you're after.

Rev Up Your Writing

Slam poetry has become a popular way for people to express themselves. Have you ever felt like expressing yourself through lyrics? Write a poem or rap describing an event in your life. Use as many of the vocabulary words as possible but make sense.

Can You Relate?

Copy this graphic organizer onto a separate piece of paper. Match the following words with their related vocabulary word. If a word relates to more than one vocabulary word, explain why.

censure When you censure people, you criticize or scold them for something they have done.

deterrent A deterrent keeps you from doing something because you are afraid of the consequences.

hindrance If something is a hindrance to you, it makes it difficult for you to do something.

malign If people malign you, they say negative and untrue things about you.

vex When you are vexed by something, you are extremely annoyed and frustrated by it.

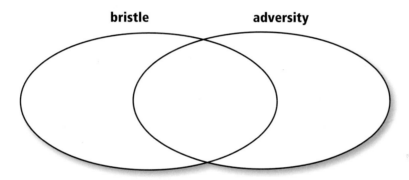
bristle　　　　adversity

In Your Own Words

Respond to one of the following prompts on a separate piece of paper. As you respond, use as many of the vocabulary words as possible. Be creative but make sense!

▶ Write about a time when you or somebody you know was treated like an outsider. Describe how this made you feel and what lesson you learned from the experience.

▶ Write an advice column that has both questions and answers for students dealing with conflict. Use details to describe the problem and advice.

▶ Write about a topic of your choice.

VOCABULARY

narcissistic
enunciate
invariably
graphically
intone
disposition
exclusion
distinct
adversity
bristle

Meeting Myself in a Museum

By Audrey Niffenegger
Illustrated by Judith Hunt

Henry has suffered all his life from a condition that makes him travel randomly backward and forward through time. In this novel excerpt, young Henry travels forward in time and meets someone very unusual.

When I get there all is quiet and still. . . . I have no idea what time it is, or how long I have to wait. . . . Time passes, nothing happens. At last: I hear a soft thud, a gasp. Silence. I wait. I stand up, silently, and pad into the Hall, walking slowly through the light that slants across the marble floor. I stand in the center of the doors and call out, not loud: "Henry."

Nothing. Good boy, wary and silent. I try again. "It's okay, Henry. I'm your guide, I'm here to show you around. It's a special tour. Don't be afraid, Henry."

I hear a slight, oh-so-faint noise. "I brought you a T-shirt, Henry. So you won't get cold while we look at the exhibits." I can make him out now, standing at the edge of the darkness. "Here. Catch." I throw it to him, and the shirt disappears, and then he steps into the light. The T-shirt comes down to his knees. Me at five, dark spiky hair, moon pale with brown almost Slavic[1] eyes, wiry, coltish.[2] At five I am happy, cushioned in normality[3] and the arms of my parents. Everything changed, starting now.

I walk forward slowly, bend toward him, speak softly. "Hello. I'm glad to see you, Henry. Thank you for coming tonight."

"Where am I? Who are you?" His voice is small and high, and echoes a little off the cold stone.

"You're in the Field Museum.[4] I have been sent here to show you some things you can't see during the day. My name is also Henry. Isn't that funny?"

He nods.

. . . "Is there anything you'd like to see first?" He shakes his head. "Tell you what. Let's go up to the third floor; that's where they keep all the stuff that isn't on display. Okay?"

"Okay."

We walk through darkness, up the stairs. He isn't moving very fast, so I climb slowly with him. . . .

". . . how did I get here?" He stops at the top of the stairs and looks at me with total confusion.

"Well, that's a secret. If I tell you, you have to swear not to say anything to anyone."

FOOTNOTES
1 *Slavic:* people of central or Eastern Europe
2 *coltish:* playful
3 *cushioned in normality:* safe in a familiar place
4 *Field Museum:* a natural history museum in Chicago

"Why?"

"Because they wouldn't believe you. You can tell Mom, or Kimy if you want, but that's it. Okay?"

"Okay. . . ."

I kneel in front of him, my innocent self, look him in the eyes. "Cross your heart and hope to die?"

"Uh-huh. . . ."

"Okay. Here's how it is: you time traveled. You were in your bedroom, and all of a sudden, poof! you are here, and it's a little earlier in the evening, so we have plenty of time to look at everything before you have to go home." He is silent and quizzical. "Does that make sense?"

"But . . . why?"

"Well, I haven't figured that out yet. I'll let you know when I do. In the meantime, we should be moving along. . . ."

. . . We walk slowly down the corridor. I decide to experiment. "Let's try this one." I slide the bookmark along a door marked *306* and open it. When I flick on the lights there are pumpkin-sized rocks all over the floor, whole and halved, craggy[5] on the outside and streaked with veins of metal inside. "Ooh, look, Henry. Meteorites."

"What's meterites?"

"Rocks that fall from outer space." He looks at me as though I'm from outer space. "Shall we try another door?" He nods. I close the meteorite room and try the door across the corridor. This room is full of birds. Birds in simulated flight, birds perched eternally on branches, bird heads, bird skins. I open one of the hundreds of drawers; it contains a dozen glass tubes, each holding a tiny gold and black bird with its name wrapped around a foot. Henry's eyes are the size of saucers. "Do you want to touch one?"

"Uh-huh."

I remove the cotton wadding from the mouth of a tube and shake a goldfinch onto my palm. It remains tube-shaped. Henry strokes its small head, lovingly. "It's sleeping?"

"More or less." He looks at me sharply, distrusting my equivocation. . . . I lead the way out into the hall, and suddenly I recollect what it was I loved about this night when I was little.

"Hey, Henry. Let's go to the library." He shrugs. I walk, quickly now, and he runs to keep up. The library is on the third floor, at the east end of the building. . . .

FOOTNOTES
....
[5] *craggy:* rough or rugged

"*Entrez!*"[6] I hold open the door and he walks in. I flip on the lights and the Reading Room springs into being. . . .[7] There are bookcases lining the room, but they hold mostly leather-bound Victorian science periodicals. The book I'm after is in a huge glass and oak case by itself in the center of the room. . . . I walk behind the Reference Desk and find a piece of felt and some support pads, and lay them out on the nearest table. Then I close and carefully lift the book out of its case and onto the felt. I pull out a chair. "Here, stand on this so you can see better." He climbs up, and I open the book.

It's Audubon's *Birds of America,* the deluxe, wonderful double-elephant folio[8] that's almost as tall as my young self. This copy is the finest in existence, and I have spent many rainy afternoons admiring it. I open it to the first plate, and Henry smiles, and looks at me.
" '*Common Loon,*' " he reads. "It looks like a duck."

"Yeah, it does. I bet I can guess your favorite bird."
He shakes his head and smiles. . . .
I open the book to *Flamingo.* Henry laughs.
"Am I right?"
"Yes!"
It's easy to be omniscient when you've done it all before. . . .

Turning each page is like making a bed, an enormous expanse of paper slowly rises up and over. Henry stands attentively, waits each time for the new wonder, emits small noises of pleasure for each sandhill crane, American coot, great auk, pileated woodpecker. When we come to the last plate, *Snow Bunting,* he leans down and touches the page, delicately stroking the engraving. I look at him, look at the book, remember, this book, this moment, the first book I loved, remember wanting to crawl into it and sleep.
"You tired?"
"Uh-huh."
"Should we go?"
"Okay."
I close *Birds of America,* return it to its glass home, open it to *Flamingo,* shut the case, lock it . . . return the felt to the desk and push the chair in. Henry turns out the light, and we leave the library.

We wander, chattering amiably of things that fly and things that slither. . . . Henry tells me about Mom and Dad and Mrs. Kim, who is teaching him to make lasagna, and Brenda, whom I had forgotten about, my best pal when I was little until her family moved to Tampa, Florida, about three months from now. We are standing in front of Bushman, the legendary silverback gorilla . . . when Henry cries out, and staggers forward, reaching urgently for me, and I grab him, and he's gone. The T-shirt is warm empty cloth in my hands. I sigh. . . . My young self will be home now, climbing into bed. I remember, I remember. I woke up in the morning and it was all a wonderful dream. Mom laughed and said that time travel sounded fun, and she wanted to try it, too.

That was the first time.

Explain Yourself

Answer each question on a separate piece of paper. Be sure to explain your answers.

1. Would you feel **wary** if your best friend walked into your classroom? Why or why not?

2. Would you expect a **wiry** person to be able to lift heavy weights? Explain.

3. Would you be **quizzical** if you heard it was snowing in Alaska? Explain.

4. Would you be afraid if you saw a **simulated** bear attack? Why or why not?

5. What occasion might make you want to **equivocate**? Why?

6. What kind of day would you want to **recollect**? Explain.

7. Would an **omniscient** person be surprised by a pop quiz? Explain.

8. What do cars **emit**? Explain.

9. Would you be **engrossed** by a television show about bugs? Why or why not?

10. Would you want to have a best friend who is very **impressionable**? Why or why not?

VOCABULARY

wary   If you are wary about something, you are worried that it might be dangerous or cause problems.

wiry   Someone who is wiry is thin but strong.

quizzical   If you are quizzical about something, you question it or doubt it.

simulate   When you simulate something, you pretend that you are doing it.

equivocate   When you equivocate, you avoid telling the truth by not giving a direct answer.

recollect   If you recollect something, you remember it.

omniscient   Someone who is omniscient knows or seems to know everything.

emit   To send out or give off something is to emit it.

engross   If something engrosses you, it takes up your full attention.

impressionable   If you are impressionable, you are easily influenced by others.

Take It Further

Complete these sentences on a separate piece of paper.

1. When I saw the principal at the skate park, I felt **wary** because . . .

2. Edward's **wiry** appearance is a result of . . .

3. I was **quizzical** when my brother said . . .

4. Marcos **simulated** driving a car by . . .

5. Politicians sometimes **equivocate** because . . .

6. Micah searched and searched for her CD until she **recollected** . . .

7. Amaya decided her mother was **omniscient** when . . .

8. Paul was shocked when the baby began to **emit** . . .

9. The play Sandra was watching was so **engrossing** that . . .

10. Because my younger sister is **impressionable**, my parents . . .

Explore It

Omniscient and *omnipresent* share the same prefix, *omni–*. **Many words are formed by combining a root word with a prefix. For example, the word** *omnipresent* **means "present all the time." So, the prefix** *omni–* **means "all." You can use this as a clue to figure out the meaning of words with the prefix** *omni–*.

Working in a small group, take what you know about the meaning of the prefix *omni–* and create other words of your own that contain the same prefix. For example, what would you call a person who is always annoying? How about a person who is always late? Have fun and be ready to share your new word creations with the class.

Bonus: List and find the meanings for real words with the prefix omni–.

Dirty Job DEBATE

My job is truly horrible; it really is a dud,
because each day I have to stomach gore and guts and blood.
I'm sure by now you're wondering what is my one great skill.
No, I'm not a murderer; I just clean up roadkill!

I know you've seen dead animals lying in the road,
bloody deer and mangled squirrels and even little toads.
While other people look away and are feeling kind of wary,
I ride in and clean things up, so the roads are much less scary.

My job is quite important, though most won't agree.
Just think of all I do for the world and then you, too, will see.
I keep all of the bodies from clogging up the streets.
So when you see me working, honk as your car retreats.

I also have a dirty job; it's worse than you might think,
because each day I have to endure smells that really stink.
I'm sure you are wondering just exactly what's my job.
Well, I have to clean up bathrooms, and it makes me
    want to sob.

An outdoor toilet cleaner is how I earn my living.
I can recollect times when this job's been unforgiving.
Day after day I go in and clean up all the mess.
    It's a thankless, dirty job; I really must confess.

Someone has to do my duty or things could
        get quite rank.
    Imagine the smells that would emit
        from the dirty toilet tank.
    Life would be unbearable if it
        weren't for my job, you see.
    So when you use an outdoor toilet,
        help keep it clean for me!

THE WORLD'S ODDEST JOBS

1 ICE CREAM TASTER

Who knew you could make a living by eating ice cream? Ice cream tasters eat small samples of ice cream to check the quality. Those with a wiry build better watch out!

2 WRINKLE CHASER

No, this job doesn't require chasing people who wear wrinkled clothes. Instead, a wrinkle chaser is a person who irons wrinkles from shoes or shoe parts. They use a special kind of iron to smooth out the shoes before they hit the stores.

3 FORTUNE COOKIE WRITER

Did you ever wonder who writes the messages inside fortune cookies? Well, a fortune cookie writer does the job, of course. Only those who can write short, clever sayings should apply.

4 SNAKE MILKER

You may know that people milk cows, but did you know that some people milk snakes? Snake milkers extract venom from poisonous snakes. The venom is then used to create cures for snakebites. So snake milkers actually work to save people's lives!

5 JOYOLOGIST

Have you ever heard that laughter is the best medicine? Joyologists would agree. A joyologist is a doctor of sorts that helps bring laughter into patients' lives. You may be quizzical about whether a joyologist is an actual profession, but it's true. So if you're ever feeling down, you know whom to call!

Rev Up Your Writing

You've read about several messy or unusual jobs. Write about a time when you or someone you know had a messy or unusual job to do. Was it enjoyable? Why or why not? Use as many of the vocabulary words as possible but make sense.

Word Organizer

Copy this graphic organizer onto a separate piece of paper.

Wary is near the hot end of the Word-O-Meter. Think of words that would be hotter or colder. Write your answers in the boxes. Explain your answers.

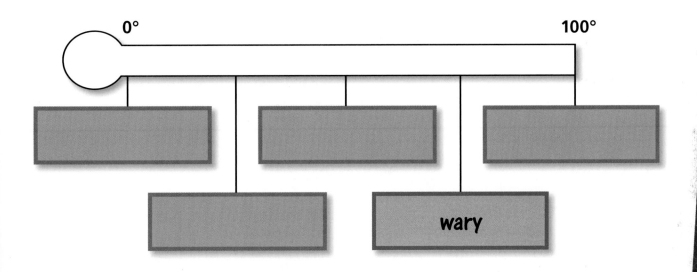

0°   100°

wary

Wacky Fortunes
Here are some strange sayings
found in fortune cookies.

Be wary of strangers giving away
used soda straws.

Help! I'm being held prisoner in
a Chinese bakery!

Follow the monkey with the flashlight.

Wild About Insects!

7:44 am (4 hours ago)

Inbox   Cockroaches

☆ Trina to Dr. Entom O. Loguez

Dear Dr. Entom O. Loguez,

My name is Trina. I am a student, and I have an assigment to write about an insect of my choice. I chose cockroaches. Can you give me any interesting facts to use in my report?

—Trina

Reply → Forward

| Send | Save Now | Discard |

To: Trina

☆ Trina,

I'm glad to hear that you're interested in my favorite bug. I don't want to equivocate; roaches are pretty disgusting. You may or may not know that cockroaches will eat absolutely anything. They'll eat grease, sweat, and even people's fingernails. If they lose a leg or a piece of their body, they'll snack on that, too! Also, cockroaches reproduce rapidly. For example, the German cockroach can have more than 500,000 offspring per year. Frightening, isn't it? But I like to think about the positive aspects of every insect. While cockroaches can be pests, they can be helpful, too. Did you know that some doctors use them for cancer research? The nerve cells in a roach's brain are a lot like ours. This makes them ideal to use for study. OK, I'll stop there. I don't want to write your report for you! As you can see, I can become engrossed in this subject. I hope these ideas will help you.

—Dr. Loguez (Dr. Bug)

Trying to Stand OUT

I'll be the first to admit that my life is pretty ordinary. Last weekend I wanted to change that by doing something crazy. I got my brilliant idea after reading about a teenager who won a contest by catching flies with chopsticks. Surely, people would remember me if I won an unusual contest!

It would've come in handy to be omniscient. I wouldn't have had to search for a contest, I'd just have known. I read every newspaper and magazine, until I finally found a contest. Our local amusement park was holding an insect-eating contest. Perfect!

I knew I could win. I just needed to practice first. My little brother is really impressionable, so it was easy to convince him to find some bugs for me to eat. We tried to simulate the conditions of the contest, but I felt sick once I saw the insects. So I decided to wait for the real thing.

I was so nervous the day of the contest. They placed a plate of insects in front of me and we were off. I picked up one cricket, closed my eyes, and shoved it in my mouth. All of a sudden, I began to gag. Before I knew it, my breakfast was on the ground in front of me. My mishap began a chain reaction. All of the other contestants began to get sick, too. Needless to say, I didn't win the contest. But, now I'm unforgettable!

Rev Up Your Writing

You've just read a couple of stories that could send even the bravest person climbing up the wall. Describe an experience you've had with an insect. What happened? Were you afraid? Use as many of the vocabulary words as possible but make sense.

Can You Relate?

Copy this graphic organizer onto a separate piece of paper. Match the following words with their related vocabulary word. If a word relates to more than one vocabulary word, explain why.

ambiguous   Something that is ambiguous is unclear.
gullible   If you are gullible, you trust and believe people too easily.
pensive   When you are pensive, you think deeply about things.
quibble   If you quibble about something, you argue about unimportant details to avoid a bigger problem.
vulnerable   If you are vulnerable, you are easily persuaded or likely to give in to temptation.

equivocate	impressionable	recollect

In Your Own Words

VOCABULARY

wary
wiry
quizzical
simulate
equivocate
recollect
omniscient
emit
engross
impressionable

Respond to one of the following prompts on a separate piece of paper. As you respond, use as many of the vocabulary words as possible. Be creative but make sense!

▶ Write about a time when you or someone you know stood out from the crowd. What made you stand out? How did you feel about yourself?

▶ Imagine that you could travel back in time and meet a younger version of yourself. Describe this meeting. What advice would you give to your younger self?

▶ Write about a topic of your choice.

Neat People vs. Sloppy People

By Suzanne Britt

Did you ever wonder why some people are organized and some people are a mess? You might be surprised by what the author thinks these qualities reveal about our true selves.

I've finally figured out the difference between neat people and sloppy people. The distinction is, as always, moral. Neat people are lazier and meaner than sloppy people.

Sloppy people, you see, are not really sloppy. Their sloppiness is merely the unfortunate consequence of their extreme moral rectitude. Sloppy people carry in their mind's eye[1] a heavenly vision, a precise plan, that is so stupendous, so perfect, it can't be achieved in this world or the next.

Sloppy people live in Never-Never Land. Someday is their métier.[2] Someday they are planning to alphabetize all their books and set up home catalogues. Someday they will go through their wardrobes and mark certain items for tentative mending and certain items for passing on to relatives of similar shape and size. Someday sloppy people will make family scrapbooks into which they will put newspaper clippings, postcards, locks of hair, and the fried corsage from their senior prom. Someday they will file everything on the surface of their desks, including the cash receipts from coffee purchases at the snack shop. Someday they will sit down and read all the back issues of *The New Yorker*.

For all these noble reasons and more, sloppy people never get neat. They aim too high and wide. They save everything, planning someday to file, order, and straighten out the world. But while these ambitious plans take clearer and clearer shape in their heads, the books spill from the shelves onto the floor, the clothes pile up in the hamper and closet, the family mementos accumulate[3] in every drawer, the surface of the desk is buried under mounds of paper and the unread magazines threaten to reach the ceiling.

Sloppy people can't bear to part with anything. They give loving attention to every detail. When sloppy people say they're going to tackle the surface of the desk, they really mean it. Not a paper will go unturned; not a rubber band will go unboxed. Four hours or two weeks into the excavation, the desk looks exactly the same, primarily because the sloppy person is meticulously creating new piles of papers with new headings and scrupulously[4] stopping to read all the old book catalogs before he throws them away. A neat person would just bulldoze the desk.

FOOTNOTES
1 *mind's eye:* imagination
2 *métier:* French word for specialty
3 *accumulate:* collect or build up
4 *scrupulously:* thoroughly and with great attention to detail

Neat people are bums and clods[5] at heart. They have cavalier attitudes toward possessions, including family heirlooms. Everything is just another dust-catcher to them. If anything collects dust, it's got to go and that's that. Neat people will toy with the idea of throwing the children out of the house just to cut down on the clutter.

Neat people don't care about process. They like results. What they want to do is get the whole thing over with so they can sit down and watch the rasslin' on TV. Neat people operate on two unvarying principles: Never handle any item twice, and throw everything away.

The only thing messy in a neat person's house is the trash can. The minute something comes to a neat person's hand, he will look at it, try to decide if it has immediate use and, finding none, throw it in the trash.

Neat people are especially vicious with mail. They never go through their mail unless they are standing directly over a trash can. If the trash can is beside the mailbox, even better. All ads, catalogs, pleas for charitable contributions, church bulletins and money-saving coupons go straight into the trash can without being opened. All letters from home, postcards from Europe, bills and paychecks are opened, immediately responded to, then dropped in the trash can. Neat people keep their receipts only for tax purposes. That's it. No sentimental salvaging of birthday cards or the last letter a dying relative ever wrote. Into the trash it goes.

Neat people place neatness above everything, even economics. They are incredibly wasteful. Neat people throw away several toys every time they walk through the den. I knew a neat person once who threw away a perfectly good dish drainer because it had mold on it. The drainer was too much trouble to wash. And neat people sell their furniture when they move. They will sell a La-Z-Boy recliner while you are reclining in it.

Neat people are no good to borrow from. Neat people buy everything in expensive little single portions. They get their flour and sugar in two-pound bags. They wouldn't consider clipping a coupon, saving a leftover, reusing plastic non-dairy whipped cream containers or rinsing off tin foil and draping it over the unmoldy dish drainer.

FOOTNOTES
5 *clods:* insensitive people

You can never borrow a neat person's newspaper to see what's playing at the movies. Neat people have the paper all wadded up and in the trash by 7:05 A.M.

Neat people cut a clean swath through the organic as well as the inorganic[6] world. People, animals, and things are all one to them. They are so insensitive. After they've finished with the pantry, the medicine cabinet, and the attic, they will throw out the red geranium (too many leaves), sell the dog (too many fleas), and send the children off to boarding school (too many scuffmarks on the hardwood floors).

FOOTNOTES
....
[6] *organic as well as the inorganic:* from nature and manmade

Explain Yourself

Answer each question on a separate piece of paper. Be sure to explain your answers.

1. If you show **rectitude**, are you likely to accept blame for a mistake? Why or why not?

2. Would you buy a new outfit for a **tentative** party? Explain.

3. Where might you find a person's **mementos**? Why?

4. If you are **meticulous** while setting the table, what will it look like when you are finished? Explain.

5. If someone called you **cavalier**, would you take that as a compliment? Why or why not?

6. If you are a **sentimental** person, what would you do with a letter from a friend? Explain.

7. If you **salvage** something, what happens to it? Explain.

8. How would you make a **swath** through a crowd of people? Explain.

9. If you do your homework **haphazardly**, do you expect to earn a good grade on it? Why or why not?

10. Would you be **satirical** when describing your best friend's work habits? Explain.

rectitude   A person with rectitude has a strong and honest personality.

tentative   If something is tentative, it is planned to happen but not certain.

memento   A memento is an object that you keep because it reminds you of a special person or occasion.

meticulous   Someone who is meticulous does things very carefully and with great attention to detail.

cavalier   A cavalier person doesn't take important situations seriously.

sentimental   Someone who is sentimental about things has tender and loving feelings about them.

salvage   If you salvage something, you save it from destruction.

swath   A swath is a long, wide strip or path.

haphazard   If something is haphazard, it is unplanned, disorganized, or messy.

satirical   Something that is satirical uses humor to show how foolish or wicked a person or idea is.

Take It Further

Complete these sentences on a separate piece of paper.

1. Amelia proved her **rectitude** to her friends by . . .

2. My plans to go to the mall after school were **tentative** because . . .

3. Nicolas considers the dog collar a **memento** because . . .

4. Our grandfather is **meticulous** about . . .

5. Patrick acted a little too **cavalierly** when . . .

6. I can tell that my sister is **sentimental** because she . . .

7. Marcie **salvaged** an awesome . . .

8. Make a **swath** up ahead so that we can . . .

9. Since Tony worked **haphazardly**, he had to . . .

10. I knew the play was **satirical** because . . .

Explore It

How much do you know about the story behind some of the words you use? For instance, did you know that *cavalier* comes from the French word for horseman? In English we use this word to say someone is smug or overly confident. This meaning developed because wealthy people or knights in France who rode horses literally looked down upon the common people.

Working with others, research the origin of one of the other vocabulary words using a dictionary, a book of word origins, or the Internet. Draw a picture that represents the word's meaning and its origin. Be ready to present your pictures to the class!

Attack of the Ballerinas

by Rhonda Arnaz

I have been studying ballet for more than ten years. Every day after school, I practice for at least two hours. It is a tiring activity, but I love it. Some people consider ballet too old-fashioned, but I disagree. I decided once and for all to prove how cool this dance form can be. (It's not just sentimental people dancing to classical music!)

Two weeks ago, I got together with some friends and we chose a hip-hop song that we liked. Then we developed the moves. We wanted to surprise people and put ballet in unexpected places around the city. That's how Ballet Attack was born!

Our first performance was Sunday afternoon at a park downtown. As a friend turned on the music, we started to dance along the swaths, so that everybody who walked by could see us. The people's responses were rather interesting. Some were a little scared because they could not figure out what was going on. Others joked cavalierly about our moves. However, I think most people enjoyed what they saw.

We plan to perform Ballet Attack at next week's talent show. Come show your support and learn something in the process!

80s Dance Party!

Pull up your leg warmers, put on a torn neon t-shirt, and tease your hair to the max because we're having a totally rad dance party!

Learn these totally awesome dances, dude!

The Egyptian
The Electric Slide
The Moon Walk
and all those super-slammin'
break dance moves!

Don't be a wannabe. Learn to dance like yo' mama did! If your moves are gnarly, you could win a glitter ball disco trophy as a memento!

**Stock up on hairspray and mascara and join us.
This event is tentatively scheduled for October 25th,
so check the Jones Gym bulletin board
for schedule changes.**

Rev Up Your Writing

The writers of the newspaper editorial and the poster were both trying to persuade their readers. Use exciting words to create an ad persuading your classmates to participate in an activity you enjoy. Use as many words as possible but make sense.

Word Organizer

Copy this graphic organizer onto a separate piece of paper.

List words that mean almost the same as *tentative* and write your answers in the web. Then tell about a time when you or someone you know acted tentatively.

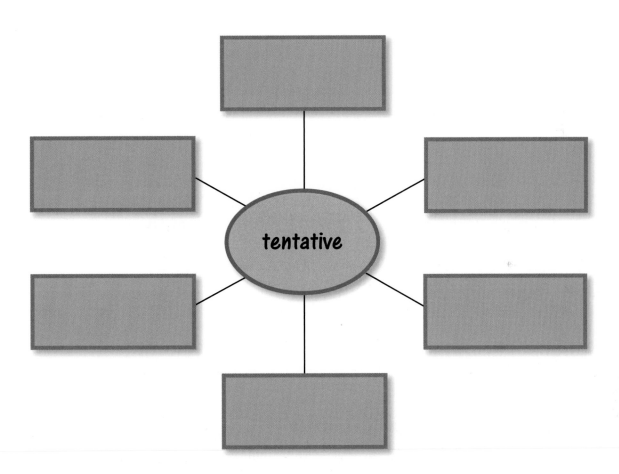

"OOPS!" Moments

Most people expect celebrities to act with dignity and rectitude. What happens when they find themselves in the most embarrassing situations? Check out the these "Oops!" Moments. Which do you think was the most embarrassing?

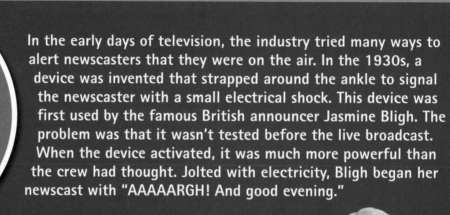

In the early days of television, the industry tried many ways to alert newscasters that they were on the air. In the 1930s, a device was invented that strapped around the ankle to signal the newscaster with a small electrical shock. This device was first used by the famous British announcer Jasmine Bligh. The problem was that it wasn't tested before the live broadcast. When the device activated, it was much more powerful than the crew had thought. Jolted with electricity, Bligh began her newscast with "AAAAARGH! And good evening."

If you've ever had a difficult time writing a long essay, then you can imagine how tough it might be to write a novel. Author Anne Rivers gets so into her work that it affects her real life. While her mind is filled with characters and plots, Rivers sometimes walks into walls. In one extreme case, she put her cat in the refrigerator and a carton of orange juice out on the back porch!

With only a few seconds left in a 1984 NBA playoff game, rookie guard Derek Harper grabbed an important rebound. Thinking his team was winning, he meticulously dribbled the ball for six seconds until the game ended. Unfortunately, Harper had forgotten to check the score, which was tied. After the buzzer sounded, the other team won the game in overtime.

For an actor, the Academy Award is possibly the most treasured prize out there. When Meryl Streep won the 1979 Award for Best Supporting Actress, she held onto the Oscar statue tightly; she even took it into the restroom with her. Unfortunately, she left it sitting on top of the toilet in the ladies restroom. Luckily, it was salvaged by a surprised guest who returned it to Streep later.

During a convention, President Truman decided to release doves into the hall as a symbol of hope. The haphazard plan misfired when the doves dive-bombed the guests, who went home with unpleasant stains on their clothes.

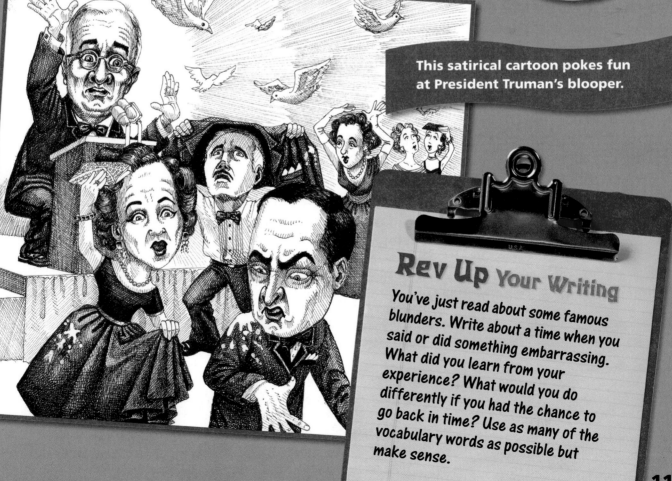

This satirical cartoon pokes fun at President Truman's blooper.

Rev Up Your Writing

You've just read about some famous blunders. Write about a time when you said or did something embarrassing. What did you learn from your experience? What would you do differently if you had the chance to go back in time? Use as many of the vocabulary words as possible but make sense.

Can You Relate?

Copy this graphic organizer onto a separate piece of paper. Match the following words with their related vocabulary word. If a word relates to several vocabulary words, explain why.

candid   Someone who is candid is open and honest.

conscientious   Conscientious people show great thought and care.

exhaustive   If you do something exhaustively, you do it thoroughly.

obsession   If you have an obsession, you focus all of your attention on only one thing.

scrupulous   If you are scrupulous, you are careful and attentive.

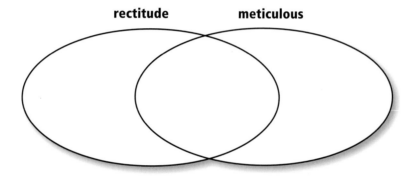

rectitude   meticulous

In Your Own Words

Respond to one of the following prompts on a separate piece of paper. As you respond, use as many of the vocabulary words as possible. Be creative but make sense!

▶ Think of a time when you or someone you know put an important task off until later. What was the end result? What did you learn from the experience?

▶ Write a poem about something special you have saved.

▶ Write about a topic of your choice.

VOCABULARY

rectitude
tentative
memento
meticulous
cavalier
sentimental
salvage
swath
haphazard
satirical

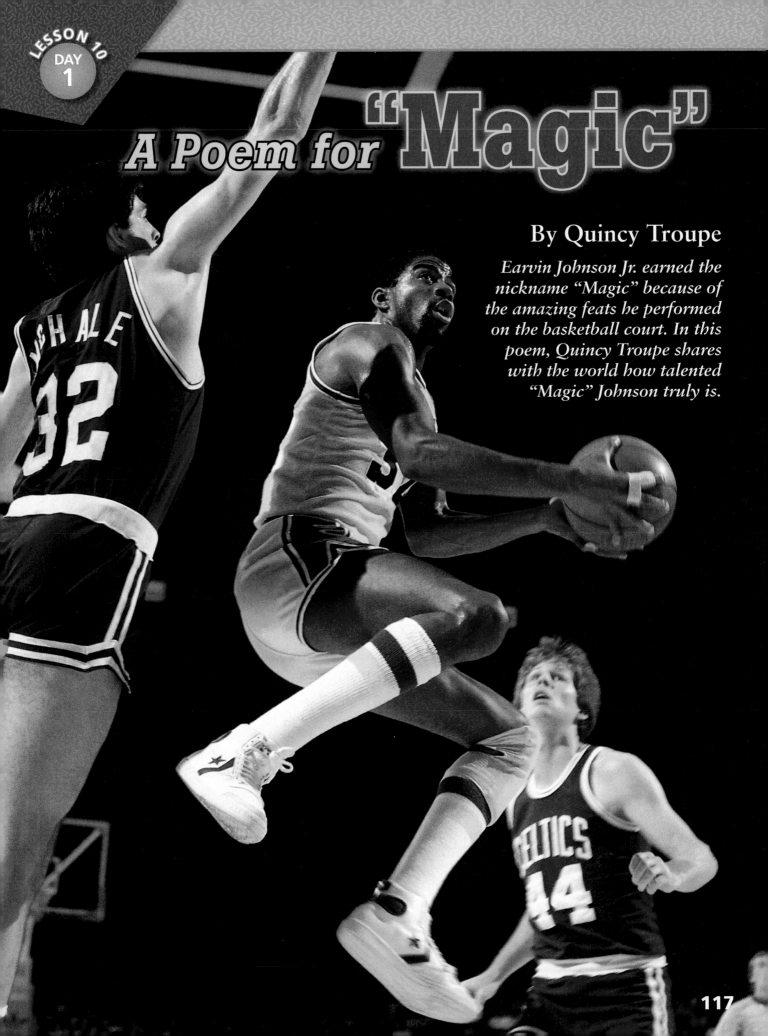

A Poem for "Magic"

By Quincy Troupe

Earvin Johnson Jr. earned the nickname "Magic" because of the amazing feats he performed on the basketball court. In this poem, Quincy Troupe shares with the world how talented "Magic" Johnson truly is.

take it to the hoop, "magic" johnson
take the ball dazzling down the open lane
herk & jerk & raise your six foot nine inch
frame into air sweating screams of your neon name
"magic" Johnson, nicknamed "windex" way back in high school
'cause you wiped glass backboards so clean[1]
where you first juked & shook
& wiled your way to glory
a new styled fusion of shake & bake energy
using everything possible you created your own space
to fly through—any moment now we expect your wings
to spread feathers for that spooky take-off of yours
then shake & glide till you hammer home
a clotheslining deuce[2] off glass
now, come back down with a reverse hoodoo gem
off the spin, & stick it in sweet popping nets
clean from twenty feet right side

put the ball on the floor, "magic"
slide the dribble behind your back, ease it deftly
between your bony stork legs, head bobbing everwhichaway
up & down, you see everything on the court, off the high
yoyo patter, stop & go dribble, you shoot
a threading needle rope pass sweet home to kareem[3]
cutting through the lane, his skyhook pops the cords
now lead the fastbreak,[4] hit jamaal[5] on the fly
now blindside a behind the back pinpointpass for two more
off the fake, looking the other way
you raise off balance into tense space
sweating chants of your name, turn 360 degrees
on the move your legs scissoring space like a swimmer's
yoyoing motion in deep water, stretching out now
towards free flight, you double pump through human trees
hang in place, slip the ball into your left hand
then deal it like a Las Vegas card dealer off squared glass
into nets living up to your singular nickname, so 'bad'[6]
you cartwheel the crowd towards frenzy
wearing now your electric smile, neon as your name

FOOTNOTES

[1] *wiped glass blackboards so clean:* caught so many rebounds

[2] *deuce:* two-point shot

[3] *kareem:* Kareem Abdul-Jabbar, who played on the Los Angeles Lakers with "Magic"

[4] *fastbreak:* players running down the court

[5] *jamaal:* Jamaal Wilkes, who played on the LA Lakers with "Magic"

[6] *bad:* cool (slang)

in victory we suddenly sense your glorious uplift
your urgent need to be champion
& so we cheer, rejoicing with you for this quicksilver, quicksilver,
    quicksilver[7]
moment of fame, so put the ball on the floor again, "magic"
juke & dazzle, shaking & baking down the lane
take the sucker to the hoop, "magic" johnson
recreate reverse hoodoo gems off the spin
deal alley-oop-dunk-a-thon-magician passes, now
double-pump, scissor, vamp through space, hang in place
& put it all in the sucker's face, "magic" johnson
& deal the roundball like the juju man that you am
like the shonuff shaman man that you am
"magic," like the shonuff spaceman you am

FOOTNOTES
....
[7] *quicksilver:* quickly
changing

Explain Yourself

VOCABULARY

Answer each question on a separate piece of paper. Be sure to explain your answers.

1. What might be hard to **wile** your friend into doing? Why?

2. Would you want to eat a **fusion** of Chinese and Italian foods? Explain.

3. Would you need to move **deftly** on a frozen pond? Why or why not?

4. What could your teacher do that would put your class into a **frenzy**? Explain.

5. What might an **urgent** phone call from a friend be about?

6. Which occupations require a person to have a lot of **fervor**? Why?

7. What would be **invigorating** after a two-hour mountain hike? Explain.

8. Which sports require athletes to be **lithe**? Why?

9. Who would you be more likely to treat with **reverence**—a younger sister or a karate instructor? Explain.

10. If you asked someone to help you, and that person gave you an **unequivocal** "no," would you ask again? Explain.

wile   Someone or something that wiles others tricks them into doing something.

fusion   Fusion is when two or more things are combined or fused together so that they can't come apart.

deftly   Something that is done deftly is done with skill and speed.

frenzy   Someone in a frenzy is so excited or nervous that he or she is nearly out of control.

urgent   If something is urgent, it needs to be taken care of immediately.

fervor   If you do something with fervor, you do it with great energy and dedication.

invigorating   Something that is invigorating makes you feel full of new energy.

lithe   A lithe person is flexible and moves gracefully.

reverence   If you have reverence for someone, you show that person deep respect.

unequivocal   If something is unequivocal, it cannot be misinterpreted because it is completely clear and obvious.

Take It Further

Complete these sentences on a separate piece of paper.

1. The magician **wiled** his audience by . . .

2. Valerie's cat looks like a **fusion** of . . .

3. If you tie a knot **deftly,** you can . . .

4. My dog went into a **frenzy** when I . . .

5. When Lena needed to send an **urgent** message she . . .

6. Larry had a **fervor** for rap music after . . .

7. Chen finds cold air **invigorating,** so he . . .

8. The monkey was so **lithe** that it . . .

9. José always acted with **reverence** when . . .

10. Sonia's answer was **unequivocal** when she said . . .

Explore It

Homonyms are words that are pronounced the same but spelled differently. For example, the words *wile* and *while* are homonyms. You've learned that to wile someone means to trick him or her. Its homonym, *while*, refers to a period of time.

With a partner, use each pair of homonyms below to make up a funny poem. Be prepared to share your wacky poem with the class!

groan/grown	guessed/guest
bored/board	weather/whether
sight/site	toad/towed

Avalanche Kills Two, Spares One

Colby Coombs survived the avalanche that took the lives of his two friends.

Mount Foraker, ALASKA—An avalanche struck experienced climbers Colby Coombs, Tom Walter, and Ritt Kellogg late in the day on June 18th, 1992.

At the time, the three climbers were using one rope to climb up the mountain. Walter lithely climbed in front, Coombs was in the middle, and Kellogg was at the end. Suddenly, an avalanche knocked the team 800 feet down the mountain, knocking Coombs unconscious.

Early on June 19th, Coombs woke up and realized he was dangling from his rope. Gripped by hypothermia, or extremely low body temperature, and extreme pain from a broken neck, ankle, and shoulder blade, he knew he needed urgent help. After releasing his rope, Coombs struggled across the snow until he managed to find his two friends. His relief soon turned to horror. Walter's face was masked with ice. He was unequivocally dead. Later, Coombs made his way down to the other climber. Kellogg hung upside down and lifeless below him.

After spending the next day getting his strength back, Coombs began the four-day trek down the mountain, mourning his lost friends and blocking out the pain. Deftly making his way across dangerous cracks and holes in the ice, Coombs finally made it to base camp on June 25th.

When Coombs was later asked to give advice to climbers who may find themselves faced with a similar situation, he explained that focusing on survival and forgetting about pain and fear are the most important skills he gained from this terrifying experience.

How Low Can You Go?

Stages of Hypothermia

Hypothermia, extremely low body temperature, has three main stages, and its effects happen gradually.

Normal Body Temperature (98.6°F)

Mild Hypothermia (94°F)

- shivering and goose bumps begin
- hands and feet become numb

As you get colder, the shivering intensifies.

Moderate Hypothermia (90°F)

- shivering is uncontrollable
- actions, like zipping a zipper are difficult
- you feel sleepy and confused
- you resist efforts to warm up

Sometimes, people who experience moderate hypothermia will take off their coats, believing that the cold is invigorating.

Severe Hypothermia (87°F)

- shivering stops
- exposed skin swells and turns blue
- actions, like walking are difficult
- muscles become stiff and you pass out

Breathing and heartbeat slow, and you die.

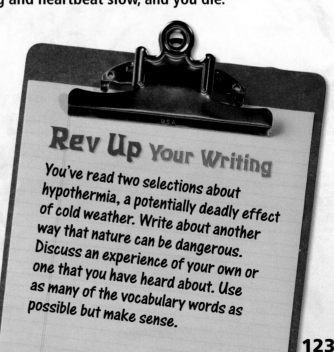

Rev Up Your Writing

You've read two selections about hypothermia, a potentially deadly effect of cold weather. Write about another way that nature can be dangerous. Discuss an experience of your own or one that you have heard about. Use as many of the vocabulary words as possible but make sense.

Word Organizer

Copy this graphic organizer onto a separate piece of paper.

Think of words that describe the word *urgent* and write your answers in the ovals. Then give examples of things that are urgent and write your answers in the boxes. Explain your answers.

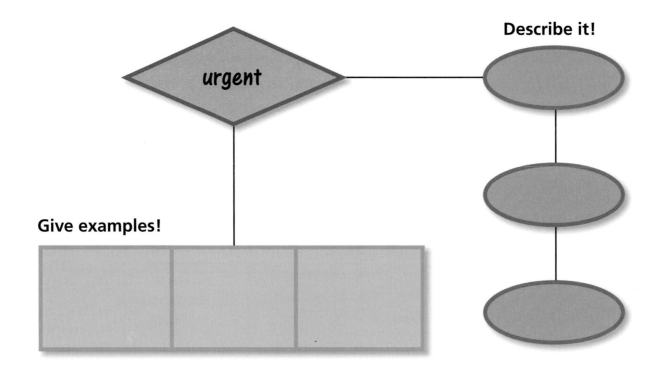

Describe it!

Give examples!

urgent

LIFE and DEATH
in the Desert

April

My Dear Babette,

DAY 3
My worst fears have come true. I am lost. I was foolish to think I could conquer the Sahara. The desert's shifting sands have wiled me into believing I was still on course.

Just now a violent windstorm swept through. The wind drove the sand into my skin like millions of tiny spears, coating my throat and making my nose bleed. I have only a few sips of water left.

DAY 5
My water is gone. Without water and food, there's no way I'll make it. The restless sand will cloak my body forever. I lie here and wait for death. I am sorry to leave you this way.

DAY 6
I awoke this morning in despair. It appears that my body is still fighting off death. I must go on. I will head for the mountain range in the distance.

DAYS 7-10
I travel only in the morning and evening. I lie in any shade I can find during midday.

DAY 11
I found a small oasis, today. Glorious water! I had a frenzied urge to drink until I became ill. I resisted. I will take all that I can carry with me.

DAY 12
Tuareg nomads found me wandering. Once on camelback, I allowed myself to believe I would see you again. I cannot express my reverence for these people.

I am alive.

Eternal Life in the Sands

The Tuareg have lived in the Sahara for thousands of years. They trade goods with travelers and provide protection for caravans. As times have changed, these desert wanderers have had to adjust, but their fervent love of the desert has helped them maintain their ancient traditions.

Tuareg people base much of their lives around their livestock; which includes camels, goats, sheep, chickens, and donkeys. Camels are important to their lifestyle, and a man's prestige is often tied to his camels.

The Tuareg are sometimes called the Blue People because they dye their cotton robes a deep blue color.

The Tuareg society is matrilineal. This means that women are responsible for passing on traditions and possessions. Women own the tents where the families live. They also compose the songs that pass history down from generation to generation.

Because of recent droughts in Africa and new policies, which don't allow the Tuareg people the freedom they once had, some Tuareg have moved to cities. Many Tuareg, however, feel they are forever fused to the nomadic lifestyle of their ancestors.

Rev Up Your Writing

What would it be like to live in the desert for a month? Describe how the environment would affect your life. Use as many of the vocabulary words as possible, but make sense.

Can You Relate?

Copy this graphic organizer onto a separate piece of paper. Match the following words with their related vocabulary word. If a word relates to more than one vocabulary word, explain why.

amalgam   An amalgam is a mixture or combination of things.
dynamic   Someone who is dynamic is full of energy and enthusiasm.
merge   If two things merge, they come together.
proficient   A person who is proficient at something is very skilled at it.
vitality   A person who is full of vitality is active and has a lot of energy.

fervor	deftly	fusion

In Your Own Words

Respond to one of the following prompts on a separate piece of paper. As you respond, use as many of the vocabulary words as possible. Be creative but make sense!

▶ Write about a time when you felt extremely excited or nervous about something. What made you feel this way? Did you keep your emotions to yourself or express yourself openly?

▶ Imagine that you write an advice column for a sports magazine. Make up a letter that an athlete might send you, and then write a response.

▶ Write about a topic of your choice.

VOCABULARY

wile
fusion
deftly
frenzy
urgent
fervor
invigorating
lithe
reverence
unequivocal

from Fighting Off the
SHARKS
for a Fish

By Gabriel García Márquez
Illustrated by Jared Osterhold

In 1955, Luis Alejandro Velasco was washed overboard the Colombian warship Caldas. The next ten days of being lost at sea would test both his survival skills and his will to survive.

I thought . . . that after seven days adrift I would become accustomed to the sea, to my anxious way of life, without having to spur my imagination in order to survive. After all, I had endured a week of harsh winds and waves. Why wouldn't it be possible to live on the raft indefinitely? The fish swam near the surface; the sea was clear and calm. There were so many lovely, tempting fish around the raft it looked as if I could grab them with my hands. Not a shark was in sight. Confidently I put my hand in the water and tried to seize a round fish, a bright blue one about twenty centimeters long. It was as if I had flung a stone: all the fish fled instantly, momentarily churning up the water. Then slowly they came back to the surface.

You have to be crafty to fish with your hand, I thought. Underwater, the hand didn't have as much strength or agility. I chose one fish from the bunch. I tried to grab it. And in fact I did. But I felt it slip through my fingers with disconcerting speed and nimbleness. I waited patiently, not pressuring myself, just trying to catch a fish. . . . But it was useless. They nibbled at my fingers, gently at first, as when they nibble at bait. Then a little harder. A smooth silver fish about a foot and a half long, with minute,[1] sharp teeth, tore the skin off my thumb. Then I realized that the nibbles of the other fish hadn't been harmless: all my fingers had small bleeding cuts.

I don't know if it was the blood from my fingers, but in an instant there was a riot of sharks around the raft. I had never seen so many. I had never seen them so voracious. They leaped like dolphins, chasing the fish and devouring them. Terrified, I sat in the middle of the raft and watched the massacre.

The next thing happened so quickly that I didn't realize just when it was that the shark leaped out of the water, thrashing its tail violently, and the raft, tottering, sank beneath the gleaming foam. In the midst of the huge, glittering wave that crashed over the side there was a metallic flash. Instinctively I grabbed an oar and prepared to strike a deathblow. But then I saw the enormous fin, and I realized what had happened. Chased by the shark, a brilliant green fish, almost half a meter long, had leaped into the raft. With all my strength I walloped it on the head with my oar. . . .

FOOTNOTES
....
[1] *minute:* very small

Little by little the water cleared and the beasts calmed down. But I had to be careful: a terrifyingly huge shark fin—the biggest I had ever seen—protruded more than a meter above the water's surface. The shark was swimming peacefully, but I knew that if it caught the scent of blood it would give a shudder that could capsize the raft. With extreme caution I began to try to pull my fish apart.

A creature that's half a meter long is protected by a hard crust of scales: if you try to pull them off, you find that they adhere to the flesh like armor plating. I had no sharp instruments. I tried to shave off the scales with my keys, but they wouldn't budge. . . .

I felt utterly frustrated and helpless at the sight of the solid, impenetrable body of the fish.

I examined it meticulously for soft spots. Finally I found a slit between the gills and with my finger I began to pull out the entrails[2]. . . .

When it was completely gutted I took the first bite. I couldn't break through the crust of scales. But on the second try, with renewed strength, I bit down desperately, until my jaw ached. Then I managed to tear off the first mouthful and began to chew the cold, tough flesh.

I chewed with disgust. I had always found the odor of raw fish repulsive, but the flavor is even more repugnant. It tastes vaguely like raw palm,[3] but oilier and less palatable. . . .

After the first piece, I felt better immediately. I took a second bite and chewed again. A moment before, I had thought I could eat a whole shark. But now I felt full after the second mouthful. The terrible hunger of seven days was appeased in an instant. I was strong again, as on the first day. . . .

I decided to wrap the fish in my shirt and store it in the bottom of the raft to keep it fresh. But first I had to wash it. Absentmindedly I held it by the tail and dunked it once over the side. But blood had coagulated[4] between the scales. It would have to be scrubbed. Naively[5] I submerged it again. And that was when I felt the charge of the violent thrust of the shark's jaws. I hung on to the tail of the fish with all the strength I had. The beast's lunge upset my balance.

FOOTNOTES
2 *entrails:* internal organs
3 *raw palm:* oil that comes from a palm tree
4 *coagulated:* thickened into an almost solid mass
5 *naively:* lacking experience

I was thrown against the side of the raft but I held on to my food supply; I clung to it like a savage. In that fraction of a second, it didn't occur to me that with another bite the shark could have ripped my arm off at the shoulder. I kept pulling with all my strength, but now there was nothing in my hands. The shark had made off with my prey. Infuriated, rabid[6] with frustration, I grabbed an oar and delivered a tremendous blow to the shark's head when it passed by the side of the raft. The beast leaped; it twisted furiously and with one clean, savage bite splintered the oar and swallowed half of it.

FOOTNOTES
[6] *rabid:* crazed or raging

Explain Yourself

Answer each question on a separate piece of paper. Be sure to explain your answers.

1. Would you expect a football player to move with **agility**? Explain.

2. Have you ever found a scene in a TV show or movie **disconcerting**? Explain.

3. Would you care if your pet had a **voracious** appetite? Why or why not?

4. Would you **devour** food that had fallen onto the floor? Why or why not?

5. What might make someone's cheeks **protrude**? Explain.

6. Would you want your school cafeteria to serve **repugnant** food? Why or why not?

7. Do you think chocolate cake is **palatable**? Explain.

8. Would you want to **appease** a school bully? Why or why not?

9. Would you expect a **dogged** person to search the entire house for a lost item? Explain.

10. Would you be **livid** if your school's soccer team won the state championship? Why or why not?

agility   Someone with agility moves with speed and skill.

disconcerting   When something is disconcerting, it is disturbing because it seems odd.

voracious   If you have a voracious appetite, you are extremely hungry and can hardly be satisfied.

devour   If you devour something, you eat it eagerly and quickly.

protrude   If something protrudes, it sticks out.

repugnant   If something is repugnant to you, you dislike it so much that it disgusts you.

palatable   Food that is palatable is acceptable to eat but not delicious.

appease   When you appease people, you give them what they want to stop them from being angry.

dogged   Someone who is dogged is determined to do something even if it is very difficult.

livid   People who are livid are extremely angry.

Take It Further

Complete these sentences on a separate piece of paper.

1. The runner's lack of **agility** caused him to . . .

2. Gertrude felt **disconcerted** when taking the test because . . .

3. Tanay could tell the dogs were **voracious** because . . .

4. Angie was surprised when she saw her dad **devour** . . .

5. José did not see the tree stump **protruding** from the ground, so . . .

6. Because the food at the restaurant was **repugnant**, Caleb . . .

7. When we told the chef his meal was **palatable**, he . . .

8. I had to **appease** my mother after I . . .

9. As a result of the detective's **dogged** investigating, she . . .

10. Coby was **livid** when . . .

Explore It

Did you know that the word *dog* can be used as a verb to mean "to follow closely and persistently like a hound"? The adjective *dogged* came from this meaning. In the English language there are many other adjectives, or describing words, that have evolved from animal names. For example:

catty: not very open or friendly

Read the sentences that describe the following words. Then, with your group, try to provide a definition for each word. Be prepared to share and explain your definitions to the class.

piggish: When Amalia sat down to dinner, she quickly began eating everything in sight.

mousy: While everyone else was enjoying the party, Jamal stood quietly in the corner.

crabby: Sabrina woke up in a bad mood. All day long she snapped at her friends and was rude to her teachers.

cowed: While all his friends couldn't wait to ride the new roller coaster, Theo looked at the ride in horror and decided to stay on the ground!

133

You Did WHAT?!

Cricket Spit

Most people would find it repugnant to hold a dead cricket in their mouths. However, Danny Capps of Madison, Wisconsin, would have to disagree. Capps holds the world record for spitting a dead cricket a whopping 30 feet!

FAST FACT!

The length of an average school bus is about 40 feet!

Squirming Worms

How much food could you eat in 30 seconds? What if the food in question is earthworms? You'd probably find this a little disconcerting, right? "Snake" Manohoran doesn't. Snake holds the record for eating 200 earthworms in 30 seconds. How did he do it? He imagined the worms were meat!

Scorpion Diet

Would you ever eat a live scorpion? If you're Rene Alvarenga from El Salvador, the answer is yes—35,000 times! Alvarenga catches 20 to 30 scorpions a day with his bare hands and devours them right on the spot!

FAST FACT!

All scorpions have venom, but only about 25 species have venom that's dangerous to humans!

Excuse Me!

Have you ever annoyed your parents by burping loudly after drinking a big glass of soda? Well, Paul Hunn's parents must have been livid whenever he burped. Hunn holds the record for the loudest burp, which measured 118 decibels!

FAST FACT!

A decibel is the unit used to measure sound. Thunder measures 120 decibels!

Flying Fish

In 2005, G.P. Vijaya Kumar accomplished an interesting feat. In one hour, he swallowed 509 small live fish and then blew each one out of his nose! It must have been quite a smelly task!

I'm Starving!

How long have you gone without eating? Probably not more than a few hours, right? Well, in 2004, Chen Jianmin went 49 days without eating a thing. To prove that his feat was not a trick, Chen lived in a glass box the entire time so that people could watch him. After 49 days with no food, Chen probably came out of that box with a voracious appetite!

Rev Up Your Writing

You've just read about people who have performed some amazing and unusual feats. Write about a time when you or someone you know did something unusual. What happened? What was so strange about it? Use as many of the vocabulary words as possible but make sense.

Word Organizer

Copy this graphic organizer onto a separate piece of paper.

List words that mean almost the same thing as *repugnant* and write your answers in the web. Then tell about a time when you smelled or ate something repugnant.

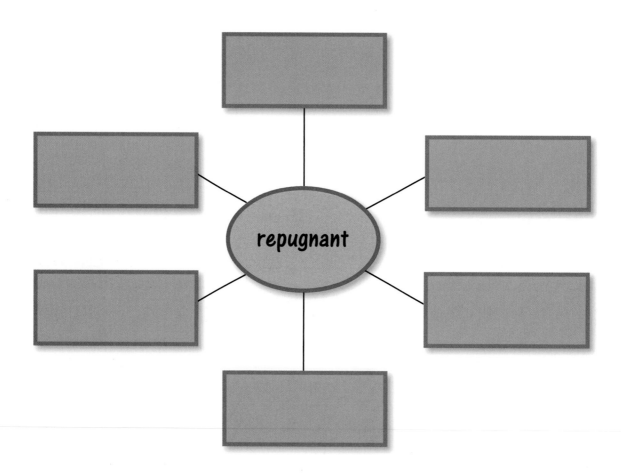

repugnant

IS IT REALLY a Sport?

You may be a sports fan, but are you hip to all the bizarre sports the world has to offer? Read the sports descriptions below. Only one of the sports is a fake. Can you guess which one it is?

1. Extreme Ironing

In this sport, adventurers iron pieces of laundry in a faraway or crazy place, such as a mountain cliff or in the middle of a busy city street!

2. World Pillow Fighting Championships

In this sport, two players sit on a slippery wet pole while holding feather pillows. The two opponents whack each other with the pillows until one player falls off the pole and into a mud pit below.

3. Underwater Hockey

In this sport, players take their hockey sticks and pucks underwater. Every few minutes the players' snorkels and masks can be seen protruding from the water.

4. Foul Food Challenge

In this sport, bakers from around the country compete to see who can make the least palatable dish. The "winner" must serve as the judge for the next year's competition!

HINT:
The number of the correct answer begins with the 6th letter of the alphabet and ends with the 18th letter of the alphabet.

Why Bowling is Not a Real Sport

a persuasive essay by Marlon Jones

A real sport is one that makes you break a sweat. A real sport requires agility, strength, and hard work. A real sport excites the spectators in the stands. Football, hockey, baseball, soccer, and basketball are all real sports. Bowling is not.

Bowling doesn't require true skill. To play, all you have to do is throw a heavy ball down a long lane and attempt to knock over a set of ten pins. Anyone can roll a ball; not everyone can hit a baseball out of the park, block a hockey puck, or make a slam dunk. These acts all require practice and talent. Bowling just requires arms, legs, eyes, and a little luck.

Sure, sports channels air bowling tournaments showing adult men and women in their dogged pursuit of a golden trophy, but think about the times when these programs come on. Mostly it's in the middle of the night when every sane person in the world is sleeping. Why do you think that is? The answer is easy: most people don't care about bowling!

Some of you may disagree with my argument, and that's OK. I'm not going to pretend to feel differently just to appease any professional bowlers I may offend. One day I might be convinced that bowling is, in fact, a sport. Until then, don't be upset with me. After all, it's only my opinion!

Rev Up Your Writing

You've just read an essay arguing that bowling is not a real sport. Do you agree or disagree? Why? Write about what you think of the author's main point and the reasons he gives to support his point. Use as many of the vocabulary words as possible but make sense.

Can You Relate?

Copy this graphic organizer onto a separate piece of paper. Match the following words with their related vocabulary word. If a word relates to more than one vocabulary word, explain why.

blanched   Someone who is blanched is white or pale because of anger, fear, or sickness.
irascible   Someone who is irascible gets angry very easily.
placid   Someone or something that is placid is very calm.
provoke   If you provoke people, you do something to make them upset.
temper   If you temper something, you make it less severe or extreme.

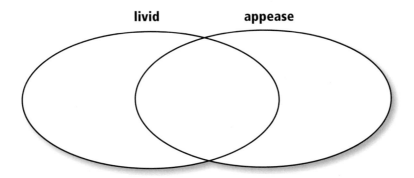

livid   appease

In Your Own Words

VOCABULARY

Respond to one of the following prompts on a separate piece of paper. As you respond, use as many of the vocabulary words as possible. Be creative but make sense!

▶ Write about an exciting or unusual trip you or someone you know has taken. Include a description of the trip and explain why it was so interesting or unusual.

▶ Imagine that you have just returned home after being stranded in the middle of the sea for two weeks. Write a memoir that describes your experiences.

▶ Write about a topic of your choice.

agility
disconcerting
voracious
devour
protrude
repugnant
palatable
appease
dogged
livid

How to Eat a Guava

By Esmeralda Santiago

Soul Food

By Janice Mirikitani

Could the foods you eat be a reflection of your identity? In this autobiographical essay and poem, the speakers describe how certain foods connect them to their culture.

How to Eat a Guava

By Esmeralda Santiago

Barco que no anda, no llega a puerto.
A ship that doesn't sail, never reaches port.

There are guavas at the Shop & Save. I pick one the size of a tennis ball and finger the prickly stem end. It feels familiarly bumpy and firm. The guava is not quite ripe; the skin is still a dark green. I smell it and imagine a pale pink center, the seeds tightly embedded in the flesh.

A ripe guava is yellow, although some varieties have a pink tinge. The skin is thick, firm, and sweet. Its heart is bright pink and almost solid with seeds. The most delicious part of the guava surrounds the tiny seeds. If you don't know how to eat a guava, the seeds end up in the crevices between your teeth.

When you bite into a ripe guava, your teeth must grip the bumpy surface and sink into the thick edible skin without hitting the center. It takes experience to do this, as it's quite tricky to determine how far beyond the skin the seeds begin.

Some years, when the rains have been plentiful and the nights cool, you can bite into a guava and not find many seeds. The guava bushes grow close to the ground, their branches laden with green then yellow fruit that seem to ripen overnight. These guavas are large and juicy, almost seedless, their roundness enticing you to have one more, just one more, because next year the rains may not come.

As children, we didn't always wait for the fruit to ripen. We raided the bushes as soon as the guavas were large enough to bend the branch.

A green guava is sour and hard. You bite into it at its widest point, because it's easier to grasp with your teeth. You hear the skin, meat, and seeds crunching inside your head, while the inside of your mouth explodes in little spurts of sour.

You grimace, your eyes water, and your cheeks disappear as your lips purse into a tight O. But you have another and then another, enjoying the crunchy sounds, the acid taste, the gritty texture of the unripe center. At night, your mother makes you drink castor oil,[1] which she says tastes better than a green guava. That's when you know for sure that you're a child and she has stopped being one.

I had my last guava the day we left Puerto Rico. It was large and juicy, almost red in the center, and so fragrant that I didn't want to eat it because I would lose the smell. All the way to the airport I scratched at it with my teeth, making little dents in the skin, chewing small pieces with my front teeth, so that I could feel the texture against my tongue, the tiny pink pellets of sweet.

Today, I stand before a stack of dark green guavas, each perfectly round and hard, each $1.59. The one in my hand is tempting. It smells faintly of late summer afternoons and hopscotch under the mango tree. But this is autumn in New York, and I'm no longer a child.

The guava joins its sisters under the harsh fluorescent lights of the exotic fruit display. I push my cart away, toward the apples and pears of my adulthood, their nearly seedless ripeness predictable and bittersweet.

FOOTNOTES
. . . .
[1] *castor oil:* a bad-tasting medicine

Soul Food

By Janice Mirikitani
For Cecil

We prepare
the meal together.
I complain,
hurt, reduced to fury[2]
again by their
subtle insults
insinuations
because I am married to you.
Impossible autonomy, no mind
of my own.

You like your fish
crisp, coated with cornmeal,
fried deep,
sliced mangos to sweeten
the tang of lemons.
My fish is raw,
on shredded lettuce,
lemon slices thin as skin,
wasabe[3] burning like green fire.
You bake the cornbread flat
and dip it in
the thick soup
I've brewed from
turkey carcass, rice gruel,
sesame oil and chervil.[4]

FOOTNOTES
[2] *reduced to fury:* angered
[3] *wasabe:* a spicy paste
made from the root of
an Asian plant
[4] *chervil:* an herb used in
cooking

We laugh over watermelon
and bubbling cobbler.

You say,
there are few men
who can stand
to have a woman equal,
upright.

This meal,
unsurpassed.

Explain Yourself

Answer each question on a separate piece of paper. Be sure to explain your answers.

1. What would you expect to be **embedded** in a wedding ring? Explain.

2. Would an outfit that has a **tinge** of color stand out in a crowd? Why or why not?

3. Is a piece of cloth **edible**? Explain.

4. Would you **purse** your lips while singing? Explain.

5. Is a squirrel an **exotic** animal? Why or why not?

6. How might you **insinuate** that someone is dishonest? Explain.

7. What are some advantages of having **autonomy**? Why?

8. Where would an **unsurpassed** athlete likely rank in a competition? Explain.

9. Do you have an **affinity** for shopping? Why or why not?

10. What might you see or hear that would **evoke** happiness? Why?

embed   If you embed something, you set it deeply inside something else.

tinge   A tinge is a small amount of something, such as color or feeling.

edible   If something is edible, it is safe to eat.

purse   If you purse your lips, you press them together tightly.

exotic   Something that is exotic is unusual and interesting because it comes from a faraway place.

insinuate   If you insinuate something, you hint that it is true without actually saying it.

autonomy   If you have autonomy, you are independent and free to make your own choices.

unsurpassed   When someone or something is unsurpassed, it is better than everything else.

affinity   If you have an affinity for someone or something, you have a natural attraction to it.

evoke   If something evokes thoughts or feelings, it brings them to mind.

Take It Further

Complete these sentences on a separate piece of paper.

1. The flower was **embedded** in . . .

2. When Monique left, Lance felt a **tinge** of . . .

3. José wanted to bring something **edible** for the hike, so he packed . . .

4. When Liz saw her father **purse** his lips, she knew . . .

5. Hakeem explained that the vase was **exotic** because . . .

6. Beatrix **insinuated** that she knew my secret by . . .

7. Yen knew her parents were giving her more **autonomy** when they . . .

8. It was obvious that Francesca's talent was **unsurpassed** when she . . .

9. William had such an **affinity** for baseball that he . . .

10. When I see these old photographs, they start to **evoke** . . .

Explore It

Many words have both synonyms and antonyms. A synonym is a word that has the same meaning. An antonym is a word that has an opposite meaning.

Get two pieces of paper. Write one of the synonyms for *affinity* on one paper, and write one of the antonyms on the other. Now listen as your partner describes a food or an event. Hold up the paper with the word that expresses how you feel about the food or event described. Have fun and be prepared to explain your answers!

What's Your COLOR?

Do you really know who you are? Are you blue, red, green, yellow, or is a tinge of every color embedded in your personality? Take this quiz and discover your true inner-self.

DIRECTIONS

Finish each sentence below by choosing the answer that best fits you. Then use the answer key on the next page to learn about the real you!

1 *You trip on the stairs in front of your whole class; you—***A.** blow it off with a joke. **B.** run to the bathroom and check yourself out. **C.** warn others to be careful. **D.** start a campaign against unsafe stairs.

2 *Someone suggests that a new student has cheated on a test; you—***A.** don't care— you just want to go outside. **B.** would think to yourself, "I would never do something like that." **C.** feel bad for him and ask him to join you for lunch. **D.** petition the school to use computers for testing.

3 *In a large party, you—***A.** are the life of the crowd. **B.** show up late because you couldn't fix your hair just right. **C.** offer to serve food and drinks. **D.** convince people to recycle their soda cans.

4 *When given a difficult school project, you—***A.** would keep your group laughing while they do the work. **B.** know that you would do a better job on your own. **C.** offer to help others who are having trouble. **D.** work with a group and make sure everyone has equal responsibility.

IF YOU CHOSE

mostly **A**s → Your color is . . . RED

mostly **B**s → Your color is . . . YELLOW

mostly **C**s → Your color is . . . BLUE

mostly **D**s → Your color is . . . GREEN

RED

PERSONALITY:
You are full of life and energy. You know how to make people smile. You use your sense of humor to get out of sticky situations.

IDEAL JOB:
You were born to be an athlete, event planner, or cheerleader.

MOTTO:
"Go for it! Life's too short."

YELLOW

PERSONALITY:
You value your autonomy and love to be in control. You need order in your life or you'll go crazy.

IDEAL JOB:
You were born to be a programmer, writer, or scientist.

MOTTO:
"Take on the world!"

BLUE

PERSONALITY:
You are an inspiration, and you don't let this go unnoticed. Your sensitivity evokes a strong desire to help others in need. Your friends can rely on you.

IDEAL JOB:
You were born to be a teacher, doctor, or social worker.

MOTTO:
"Lean on me."

GREEN

PERSONALITY:
You are influential, and your sense of justice is unsurpassed. Your friends look up to you and admire your accomplishments.

IDEAL JOB:
You were born to be an activist, politician, or environmentalist.

MOTTO:
"Save the world!"

Rev Up Your Writing

You've just taken a personality quiz. Write about whether or not you agree with the results. Use transition words when describing which aspects you agree with and which you don't. Use as many of the vocabulary words as possible but make sense.

Word Organizer

Copy this graphic organizer onto a separate piece of paper.

Write an explanation of the word *edible* in the Explain It box below. Then write a sentence using the word *edible* in the Use It box. Finally, use the Sketch It box to sketch a picture that shows the word *edible*. Explain your work.

edible **Write It**	**Explain It**
Use It	**Sketch It**

IN THEATERS NOW!

GIANT EVIL MONSTERS WHO EAT THINGS

"Giant Evil Monsters" A Giant Waste of Time

By Flicka Filmworth
MOVIE CRITIC

The new horror movie, *Giant Evil Monsters Who Eat Things*, should get eaten by giant evil monsters!

In case my insinuation is not clear enough, let me say it directly: *Giant Evil Monsters* is a terrible movie.

The only thing scary about this movie is that people might pay their hard-earned money to see it. The acting is so horrid, and the writing is so weak, you will purse your lips in anger and frustration. Even the special effects aren't great.

If you have an affinity for bad acting, clueless writing, and all-around awfulness, you will love this movie! But if you want to be spared two hours of pain and suffering, I highly recommend you avoid *Giant Evil Monsters Who Eat Things.*

Critic Flicka Filmworth raves,

"The special effects are . . . great!"

". . . people [should] pay their hard-earned money to see it!"

". . . you will love this movie!"

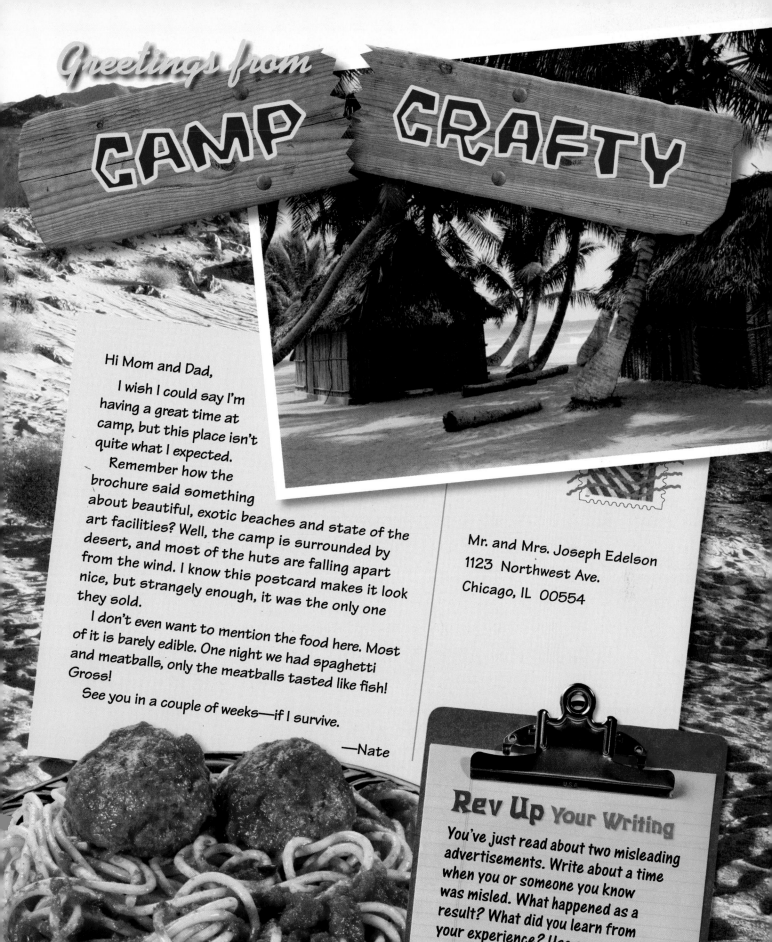

Greetings from CAMP CRAFTY

Hi Mom and Dad,

I wish I could say I'm having a great time at camp, but this place isn't quite what I expected.

Remember how the brochure said something about beautiful, exotic beaches and state of the art facilities? Well, the camp is surrounded by desert, and most of the huts are falling apart from the wind. I know this postcard makes it look nice, but strangely enough, it was the only one they sold.

I don't even want to mention the food here. Most of it is barely edible. One night we had spaghetti and meatballs, only the meatballs tasted like fish! Gross!

See you in a couple of weeks—if I survive.

—Nate

Mr. and Mrs. Joseph Edelson
1123 Northwest Ave.
Chicago, IL 00554

Rev Up Your Writing

You've just read about two misleading advertisements. Write about a time when you or someone you know was misled. What happened as a result? What did you learn from your experience? Use as many of the vocabulary words as possible but make sense.

Can You Relate?

Copy this graphic organizer onto a separate piece of paper. Match the following words with their related vocabulary word. If a word relates to more than one vocabulary word, explain why.

allude   When you allude to something, you refer to it indirectly.

elicit   When you elicit a response from others, you do or say something to get them to respond.

infallible   Someone who is infallible cannot make mistakes.

singular   If something is singular, it is remarkably good or exceptional.

subjective   If something is subjective, it is based on a personal opinion, not on facts.

insinuate	evoke	unsurpassed

In Your Own Words

VOCABULARY

embed
tinge
edible
purse
exotic
insinuate
autonomy
unsurpassed
affinity
evoke

Respond to one of the following prompts on a separate piece of paper. As you respond, use as many of the vocabulary words as possible. Be creative but make sense!

▶ Write about a time when you or a friend followed somebody's advice. What was the result? Would you listen to this person again?

▶ Imagine that you are a character from your favorite story. Write a memoir about an important moment in your life.

▶ Write about a topic of your choice.

What Is Intelligence, Anyway?

By Isaac Asimov

Have you ever met an intelligent person who didn't seem very smart?

What is intelligence, anyway? When I was in the army I received a kind of aptitude test that all soldiers took and, against a normal of 100, scored 160. No one at the base[1] had ever seen a figure like that, and for two hours they made a big fuss over me. (It didn't mean anything. The next day I was still a buck private[2] with KP[3] as my highest duty.)

All my life I've been registering scores like that, so that I have the complacent feeling that I'm highly intelligent, and I expect other people to think so, too. Actually, though, don't such scores simply mean that I am very good at answering the type of academic questions that are considered worthy of answers by the people who make up the intelligence tests—people with intellectual bents[4] similar to mine?

For instance, I had an auto-repair man once, who, on these intelligence tests, could not possibly have scored more than 80, by my estimate. I always took it for granted that I was far more intelligent than he was. Yet, when anything went wrong with my car I hastened to him with it, watched him anxiously as he explored its vitals,[5] and listened to his pronouncements as though they were divine oracles[6]—and he always fixed my car.

Well, then, suppose my auto-repair man devised questions for an intelligence test. Or suppose a carpenter did, or a farmer, or, indeed, almost anyone but an academician.[7] By every one of those tests, I'd prove myself a moron. And I'd *be* a moron, too. In a world where I could not use my academic training and my verbal talents but had to do something intricate or hard, working with my hands, I would do poorly. My intelligence, then, is not absolute[8] but is a function of the society I live in and of the fact that a small subsection of that society has managed to foist itself on the rest as an arbiter of such matters.

Consider my auto-repair man, again. He had a habit of telling me jokes whenever he saw me. One time he raised his head from under the automobile hood to say: "Doc, a deaf-and-dumb[9] guy went into a hardware store to ask for some nails. He put two fingers together on the counter and made hammering motions with the other hand.

FOOTNOTES

1 *base:* military headquarters
2 *buck private:* slang for the lowest ranking army soldier
3 *KP:* kitchen patrol
4 *bents:* natural talents for something
5 *vitals:* important parts
6 *divine oracles:* statements from God
7 *academician:* scholar
8 *absolute:* complete or perfect
9 *deaf-and-dumb:* unable to speak or hear

The clerk brought him a hammer. He shook his head and pointed to the two fingers he was hammering. The clerk brought him nails. He picked out the sizes he wanted, and left. Well, Doc, the next guy who came in was a blind man. He wanted scissors. How do you suppose he asked for them?"

Indulgently, I lifted my right hand and made scissoring motions with my first two fingers. Whereupon my auto-repair man laughed raucously and said, ". . . he used his *voice* and asked for them." Then he said, smugly, "I've been trying that on all my customers today." "Did you catch many?" I asked. "Quite a few," he said, "but I knew for sure I'd catch *you*." "Why is that?" I asked. "Because you're so . . . educated, Doc, I *knew* you couldn't be very smart."

And I have an uneasy feeling he had something there.

Explain Yourself

VOCABULARY

Answer each question on a separate piece of paper. Be sure to explain your answers.

1. How can you tell if someone has an **aptitude** for sports? Explain.

2. When might it be dangerous to be **complacent**? Explain.

3. What **pronouncement** would you like to hear the President of the United States make? Explain.

4. Would it be easy to follow a movie with an **intricate** plot? Why or why not?

5. What things would you like your parents to **foist** on you? Explain.

6. What traits would you need to be a successful **arbiter**? Explain.

7. If someone were **indulgent** toward you, would you be happy? Explain.

8. Would you act **raucously** to impress someone you like? Why or why not?

9. What might you do to **dupe** a sibling into doing your chores? Explain.

10. How would you feel if your interests and your best friend's interests were becoming **divergent**? Why?

aptitude   Aptitude is the natural ability to learn something quickly and do it well.

complacent   If you are complacent, you don't think that you need to worry or do anything about a situation.

pronouncement   Pronouncements are formal orders or announcements.

intricate   Something that is intricate is complicated or difficult because it has many details or small parts.

foist   If you foist something on people, you force it on them.

arbiter   An arbiter is someone who settles disagreements.

indulgent   If you are indulgent, you enjoy giving others whatever they want.

raucous   Something that is raucous is loud and rowdy.

dupe   When you dupe others, you fool or trick them.

divergent   Things that are divergent become more and more different from each other over time.

Take It Further

Complete these sentences on a separate piece of paper.

1. The dog had a low **aptitude** and couldn't . . .

2. Because the singer was **complacent**, he . . .

3. The students were nervous after the **pronouncement** that . . .

4. Because his new game had **intricate** directions, Carlos . . .

5. Although it was an accident, Aubrey still got upset when Gabe **foisted** . . .

6. My friends and I needed an **arbiter** after we . . .

7. Brian behaved **indulgently** toward Tessa because . . .

8. The students acted **raucously** when . . .

9. The magician **duped** the audience by . . .

10. Roy and Alejandro had **divergent** opinions on what to watch, so they . . .

Explore It

One word can take many different forms. You already know the word *indulgent,* an adjective that describes someone who enjoys giving others whatever they want. This word comes from *indulge,* a verb that means "to let someone else or yourself have or do something fun." Other words in this word family are *indulgence,* a noun that means "a luxury that somebody lets himself or herself have," and *indulgently,* an adverb that means "in a generous and giving way."

Working with a partner, create a comic strip in which the main character likes to indulge others. Be sure to show the character acting indulgently and describe what indulgences he or she likes to give others. Use at least two of the words in the comic strip, and be prepared to share your comic with the class!

Flawed Laws

Since the early days of our country, the government has foisted many laws on the public. Most laws are passed to keep people safe. But did you know that many states have laws that might have made sense once, but are now outdated? Below are some examples of the country's most unusual laws.

Weird Animal Laws

In Little Rock, Arkansas, dogs can't indulge in any behavior they choose. For example, in this city, dogs are not permitted to bark after 6:00 P.M.

If you are in Michigan and feel like tying a crocodile to a fire hydrant, forget it! This behavior is forbidden.

For California hunters, lawmakers have made a very interesting pronouncement. You are not allowed to hunt any kind of animal while riding in a moving vehicle, unless, of course, you are hunting by sea!

In Seattle, Washington, it is illegal for a goldfish to ride on a bus—unless it lies still!

Brooklyn, New York, listen up! If your donkey gets tired, steer clear of the bathroom. You wouldn't want your donkey to fall asleep in the bathtub—it's illegal!

NO PARKING AFTER 6:00 PM

Weird People Laws

If you buy a home in Garfield County, Montana, avoid drawing intricate portraits on your window shades. Unless, of course, you want to break the law.

When you have a family picnic, do conversations sometimes get so loud and rowdy that an arbiter is needed to come in and calm things down? Well, don't have a picnic in Pennsylvania anytime soon. A Pennsylvania law forbids loud talking at picnics.

Laws are usually passed to keep criminals off the street. However, in Kulpmont, Pennsylvania, there is a law on record that may help reverse that process. The law states that it is illegal to keep a prisoner in jail on Sunday!

If you live in Atlanta, Georgia, and don't like to bathe, consider this: it is illegal for a smelly person to ride on a streetcar!

Do you like to sing every once in a while? Well, go ahead—sing away! But if you're in North Carolina, you'd better stay in tune. It's the law!

Rev Up Your Writing

You've just read about many strange laws. Write about some unusual laws you would you like to see passed in your state. Why do you think your state needs such laws? Use as many of the vocabulary words as possible but make sense.

Word Organizer

Copy this graphic organizer onto a separate piece of paper.

List things that are raucous in the top half of the Word Wheel. List things that are not raucous in the bottom half.

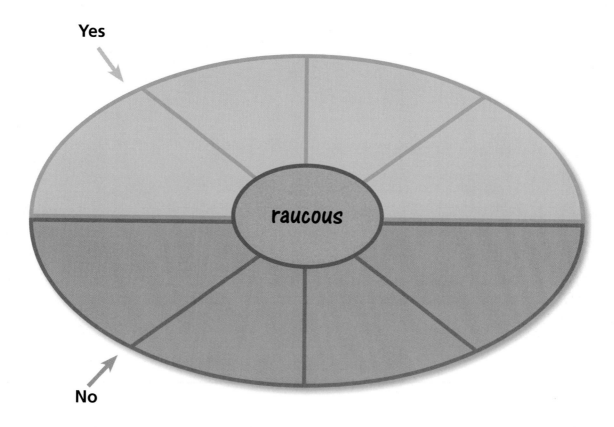

Yes

raucous

No

Lucky New Year!

Different countries and cultures have divergent New Year's traditions, but most have one important thing in common: starting the year in the best way possible. Here are traditions meant to dupe bad luck into staying away all year long.

China

In China, the character *fu* means "luck." The same character upside down asks for luck to arrive. Chinese families paint red and gold signs with this character on them and hang them upside down until New Year's Day, hoping that good luck will arrive in the new year.

Spain

If you want to have good luck in Spain, you'd better like grapes. The Spanish eat twelve grapes at midnight on New Year's Eve to ensure twelve good months.

Japan

Japanese families laugh raucously at midnight on New Year's Eve so that they will be happy all year long.

Scotland

Tall, dark, and handsome men get lots of party invitations for the New Year in Scotland. It's especially lucky if one of these fine gentlemen is the first to enter your house on New Year's Day.

161

Come Be a Polar Bear!

Date: January 1
Time: 12:00 P.M.
Place: Lakeside Waterfront, Center Street entrance

If you have an aptitude for swimming and want a chilly thrill, come join the Lakeside Polar Bear Club for the 20th Annual New Year's Day Swim. What better way to ring in the New Year than jumping into icy cold Lake Michigan?

Be sure to bring your swimsuit, and don't be complacent about the cold even though you will be swimming through ice. Water shoes and warm clothes for afterward are required.

Hot cocoa and warm goodies will be served.

Rev Up Your Writing

You've just read about strange traditions that take place around the world. Write about an unusual tradition that you've heard of. Why is this tradition unusual? Use as many of the vocabulary words as possible but make sense.

Can You Relate?

Copy this graphic organizer onto a separate piece of paper. Match the following words with their related vocabulary word. If a word relates to more than one vocabulary word, explain why.

chicanery   If you use chicanery, you use words to trick or mislead others.

compel   If you compel someone to do something, you force him or her to do it.

evade   If you evade someone, you get away from him or her by using trickery.

finesse   If you have finesse, you use a skillful approach when dealing with a difficult situation.

vehement   If you are vehement, you are very forceful.

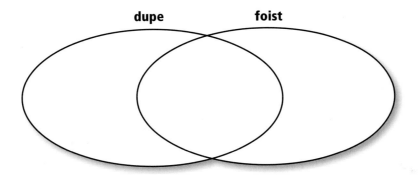

dupe   foist

In Your Own Words

Respond to one of the following prompts on a separate piece of paper. As you respond, use as many of the vocabulary words as possible. Be creative but make sense!

▶ Write about a time when your first impression of someone turned out to be wrong. Explain how he or she turned out to be different than you expected.

▶ Think about a strange event or activity that you have read about or participated in. Write a letter to a friend that describes this event or activity.

▶ Write about a topic of your choice.

VOCABULARY

aptitude
complacent
pronouncement
intricate
foist
arbiter
indulgent
raucous
dupe
divergent

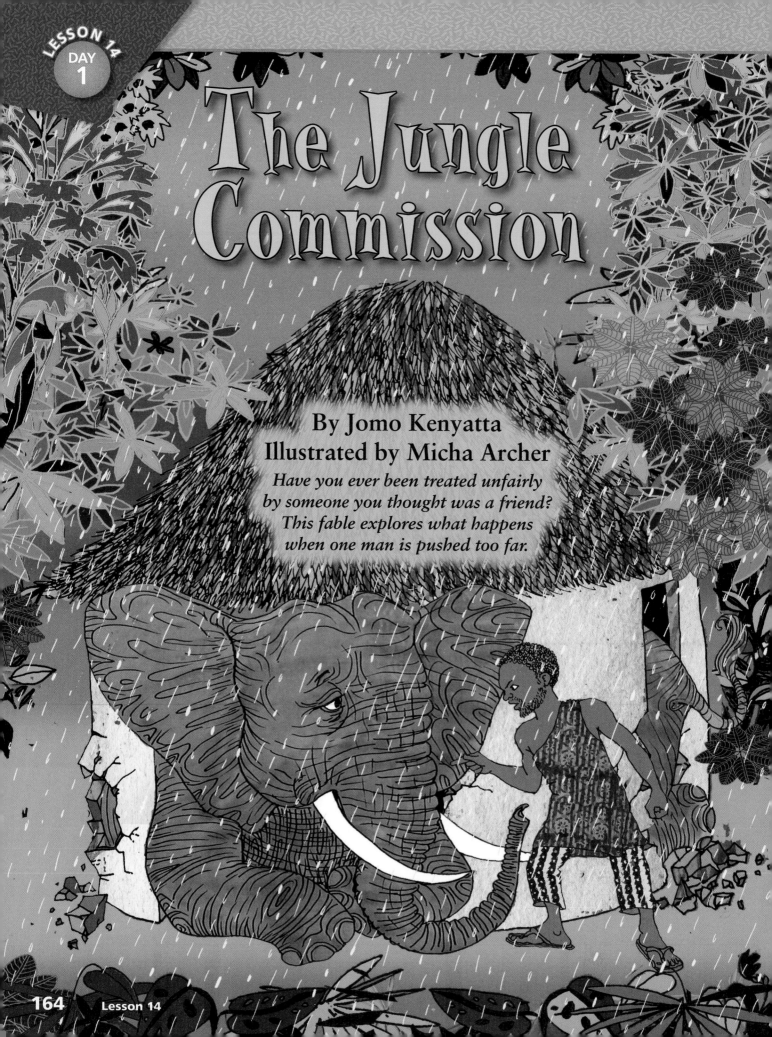

The Jungle Commission

By Jomo Kenyatta
Illustrated by Micha Archer
*Have you ever been treated unfairly
by someone you thought was a friend?
This fable explores what happens
when one man is pushed too far.*

The relation between the Gikuyu[1] and the Europeans can well be illustrated by a Gikuyu story which says: That once upon a time an elephant made a friendship with a man. One day a heavy thunderstorm broke out, the elephant went to his friend, who had a little hut at the edge of the forest, and said to him: "My dear good man, will you please let me put my trunk inside your hut to keep it out of this torrential rain?" The man, seeing what situation his friend was in, replied: "My dear good elephant, my hut is very small, but there is room for your trunk and myself. Please put your trunk in gently." The elephant thanked his friend, saying: "You have done me a good deed and one day I shall return your kindness." But what followed? As soon as the elephant put his trunk inside the hut, slowly he pushed his head inside, and finally flung the man out in the rain, and then lay down comfortably inside his friend's hut, saying: "My dear good friend, your skin is harder than mine, and as there is not enough room for both of us, you can afford to remain in the rain while I am protecting my delicate skin from the hailstorm."

The man, seeing what his friend had done to him, started to grumble; the animals in the nearby forest heard the noise and came to see what was the matter. All stood around listening to the heated argument between the man and his friend the elephant. In this turmoil the lion came along roaring, and said in a loud voice: "Don't you all know that I am the King of the Jungle! How dare anyone disturb the peace of my kingdom?" On hearing this the elephant, who was one of the high ministers[2] in the jungle kingdom, replied in a soothing voice, and said: "My Lord, there is no disturbance of the peace in your kingdom. I have only been having a little discussion with my friend here as to the possession of this little hut which your lordship sees me occupying." The lion, who wanted to have "peace and tranquility" in his kingdom, replied in a noble voice, saying:

FOOTNOTES
1 *Gikuyu:* culture of Kenya, Africa.
2 *high ministers:* important member of a government

165

"I command my ministers to appoint a Commission of Enquiry to go thoroughly into this matter and report accordingly." He then turned to the man and said: "You have done well by establishing friendship with my people, especially with the elephant who is one of my honorable ministers of state. Do not grumble any more, your hut is not lost to you. Wait until the sitting of my Imperial Commission, and there you will be given plenty of opportunity to state your case. I am sure that you will be pleased with the findings of the Commission." The man was very pleased by these sweet words from the King of the Jungle, and innocently waited for his opportunity, in the belief that, naturally, the hut would be returned to him.

The elephant, obeying the command of his master, got busy with other ministers to appoint the Commission of Enquiry. The following elders of the jungle were appointed to sit in the Commission: (1) Mr. Rhinoceros; (2) Mr. Buffalo; (3) Mr. Alligator; (4) The Rt. Hon.[3] Mr. Fox to act as chairman; and (5) Mr. Leopard to act as Secretary to the Commission. On seeing the personnel, the man protested and asked if it was not necessary to include in this Commission a member from his side. But he was told that it was impossible, since no one from his side was well enough educated to understand the intricacy of jungle law. Further, that there was nothing to fear, for the members of the Commission were all men of repute[4] for their impartiality in justice, and as they were gentlemen chosen by God to look after the interests of races less adequately endowed[5] with teeth and claws, he might rest assured that they would investigate the matter with the greatest care and report impartially.

The Commission sat to take the evidence. The Elephant was first called. He came along with a superior air,[6] brushing his tusks with a sapling which Mrs. Elephant had provided, and in an authoritative voice said: "Gentlemen of the Jungle, there is no need for me to waste our valuable time in relating a story which I am sure you all know. I have always regarded it as my duty to protect the interests of my friends, and this appears to have caused the misunderstanding between myself and my friend here. He invited me to save his hut from being blown away by a hurricane. As the hurricane had gained access owing to the unoccupied space in the hut, I considered it necessary, in my friend's own interests, to turn the undeveloped space to a more economic use by sitting in it myself; a duty which any of you would undoubtedly have performed with equal readiness in similar circumstances."

FOOTNOTES
3 *Rt. Hon.:* short for Right Honorable which is a title of respect
4 *repute:* good reputation
5 *endowed:* supplied
6 *superior air:* an arrogant attitude

After hearing the Rt. Hon. Mr. Elephant's conclusive evidence, the Commission called Mr. Hyena and other elders of the jungle, who all supported what Mr. Elephant had said. They then called the man, who began to give his own account of the dispute. But the Commission cut him short,[7] saying: "My good man, please confine yourself to relevant issues. We have already heard the circumstances from various unbiased[8] sources; all we wish you to tell us is whether the undeveloped space in your hut was occupied by anyone else before Mr. Elephant assumed his position?" The man began to say: "No, but—" But at this point the Commission declared that they had heard sufficient evidence from both sides and retired to consider their decision. After enjoying a delicious meal at the expense of the Rt. Hon. Mr. Elephant, they reached their verdict, called the man, and declared as follows: "In our opinion this dispute has arisen through a regrettable misunderstanding due to the backwardness of your ideas. We consider that Mr. Elephant has fulfilled his sacred duty of protecting your interests. As it is clearly for your good that the space should be put to its most economic use, and as you yourself have not yet reached the stage of expansion which would enable you to fill it, we consider it necessary to arrange a compromise to suit both parties. Mr. Elephant shall continue his occupation of your hut, but we give you permission to look for a site where you can build another hut more suited to your needs, and we will see that you are well protected."

The man, having no alternative, and fearing that his refusal might expose him to the teeth and claws of members of the Commission, did as they suggested. But no sooner had he built another hut than Mr. Rhinoceros charged in with his horn lowered and ordered the man to quit. A Royal Commission was again appointed to look into the matter, and the same finding was given. This procedure was repeated until Mr. Buffalo, Mr. Leopard, Mr. Hyena, and the rest were all accommodated with new huts. Then the man decided that he must adopt an effective method of protection, since Commissions of Enquiry did not seem to be of any use to him. He sat down and said: "Ng'enda thi ndeagaga motegi," which literally means "there is nothing that treads on the earth that cannot be trapped," or in other words, you can fool people for a time, but not forever.

FOOTNOTES
....
[7] *cut him short:* interrupted him
[8] *unbiased:* fair

Early one morning, when the huts already occupied by the jungle lords were all beginning to decay and fall to pieces, he went out and built a bigger and better hut a little distance away. No sooner had Mr. Rhinoceros seen it than he came rushing in, only to find that Mr. Elephant was already inside, sound asleep. Mr. Leopard next came in at the window, Mr. Lion, Mr. Fox, and Mr. Buffalo entered the doors, while Mr. Hyena howled for a place in the shade and Mr. Alligator basked[9] on the roof. Presently they all began disputing about their rights of penetration, and from disputing they came to fighting, and while they were all embroiled together the man set the hut on fire and burnt it to the ground, jungle lords and all. Then he went home, saying: "Peace is costly, but it's worth the expense," and lived happily ever after.

FOOTNOTES
9 *basked:* stretched out

Explain Yourself

Answer each question on a separate piece of paper. Be sure to explain your answers.

1. What might cause **turmoil** in your school?

2. Would you show **impartiality** if two of your friends were fighting? Explain.

3. Would you describe your grandmother as an **authoritative** person? Why or why not?

4. Do you always get **conclusive** results from a science experiment? Explain.

5. When might someone **confine** a pet?

6. Would describing how a ball is made be **relevant** during the broadcast of a soccer game? Why or why not?

7. Would you **accommodate** a friend who asked to share your lunch? Explain.

8. Write about a time when you or someone you know was **embroiled** in something.

9. Would you like it if a community college **annexed** your school? Why or why not?

10. What might cause a salesperson to become **disgruntled**?

VOCABULARY

turmoil Things are in turmoil when they are confused and out of order.

impartiality Someone who acts with impartiality acts fairly and does not favor one side over another.

authoritative An authoritative person is powerful and knowledgeable.

conclusive If something is conclusive, it is final or certain.

confine A person who is confined to a place is kept from leaving it.

relevant If something is relevant, it is connected to what is being talked about at the time.

accommodate If you accommodate others, you give them what they need or want.

embroil If you are embroiled in something, you are mixed up in something bad, such as a fight.

annex When a place has been annexed, it has been taken over.

disgruntled If you are disgruntled, you are angry and dissatisfied.

Take It Further

Complete these sentences on a separate piece of paper.

1. The inside of Solana's locker was in **turmoil** because . . .

2. I knew I couldn't be **impartial** because the disagreement was between . . .

3. The coach was not **authoritative**, so the players . . .

4. The election results were not **conclusive**, so the principal . . .

5. The teacher told me to **confine** the questions I asked her to . . .

6. The science teacher said that Jake's comment was not **relevant** because . . .

7. The hotel **accommodated** pets, so the Flores family . . .

8. The two mountain hikers became **embroiled** in . . .

9. When our teacher **annexed** the library, the librarian . . .

10. Charles became **disgruntled** when his parents told him that . . .

Explore It

You know the word *embroil* by now, but are you familiar with two words that have related meanings, *implicate* and *mire*?

implicate

If you are implicated in something, you are shown to be involved in it.

mire

If you are mired in something, you are stuck in it.

Working with someone else, decide which of the three words would fit best in the blanks in the paragraph below.

When the principal asked Sarah to tell him who had broken the school's statue, she had no choice but to 1. _____ Ivan. After all, Sarah had seen Ivan standing near the statue before it was broken. Sarah just wanted to answer the principal's questions and quickly leave his office. She didn't have time to be 2. _____ in a situation that had nothing to do with her. She felt bad for Ivan, though. He was her best friend. When he found out that she was the one who told on him, she knew that they would be 3. _____ in a fight.

Young Inventors

Reality TV

While some biographers claim that Vladimir Zworykin is the inventor of TV, others argue that it was actually Philo Farnsworth, a 14-year-old Idaho farm boy who sketched diagrams of early TV technology before Vladimir got his start. Farnsworth was the first to conclusively demonstrate a working TV transmission at the age of 21, a full five years before Zworykin. While Zworykin was the first to patent the technology, many agree that Farnsworth is TV's true father.

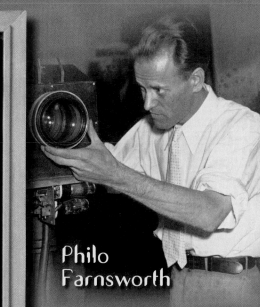

Philo Farnsworth

Brilliant!

In 1873, 15-year-old Chester Greenwood was tired of trying to keep his ears warm while ice-skating. He had tried wrapping a scarf around his head, but it felt too itchy and kept getting in the way. He asked his grandmother to sew bits of fur to loops of wire . . . have you guessed Chester's invention yet? If you answered "earmuffs," then you are correct! Chester's creation is still keeping people warm today!

How to Get a Patent

- Do the research. Find out how many other (if any) inventions there are that are similar to yours.
- Describe it. Write down exactly what your invention is and how it accommodates people's lives. Try to confine your descriptions to only the necessary information.
- Do the paperwork. Fill out an application. These can be found on the U. S. Patent and Trademark Office Web site. Make sure that you have an impartial adult help you with this step.

Thomas Edison

American Inventor

Age 7—Thomas Edison was such a bad student that his mother took him out of school and taught him at home herself.

Age 12—Edison began working as a newspaper and candy salesman on the Grand Trunk Railroad.

Age 15—Edison was going deaf. Despite this, he learned Morse code and worked as a telegraph operator for many years.

Age 19—Edison patented his first invention: the electrical vote recorder (an invention well ahead of its time!).

Age 30—Edison invented the phonograph, the first-ever sound recording device.

Do You Have What it Takes to be an Inventor?

Are you:

curious?   creative?

persistent?

a problem solver?

willing to tinker with your ideas?

If you said "yes" to four or more of the above traits, annex a garage for your new laboratory and get to work!

Rev Up Your Writing

You've just read about some inventors and their inventions. If you had all the supplies you needed, what would you invent? Why would your invention be worth patenting? Use as many of the vocabulary words as possible but make sense.

Word Organizer

Copy this graphic organizer onto a separate piece of paper.

List words that are synonyms of *authoritative*. Write your answers in the Synonyms box. Use some of the words in this box to describe a movie character that you think is authoritative.

Then list words that are antonyms of *authoritative*. Write your answers in the Antonyms box. Use some of the words to describe a movie character that you think is weak.

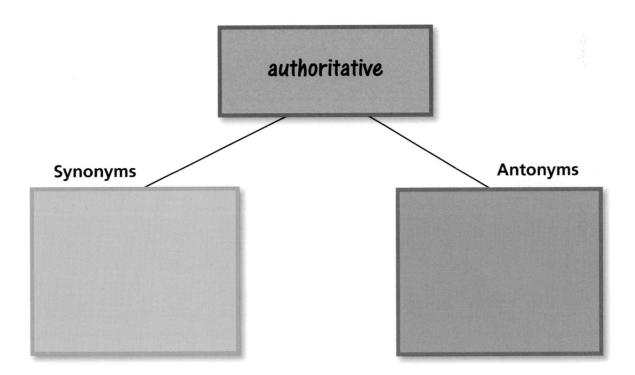

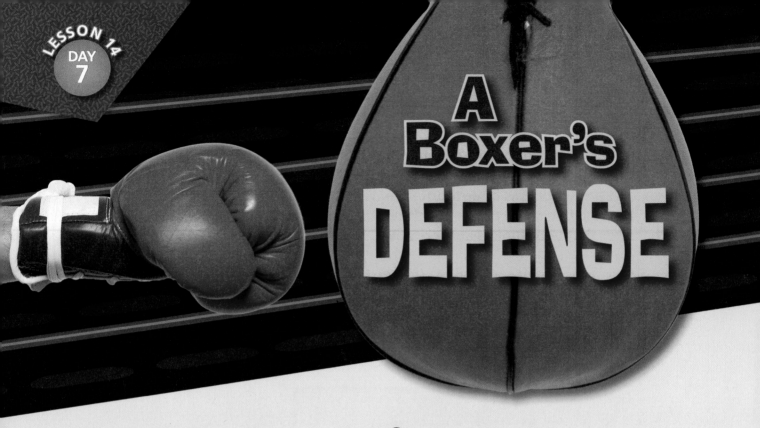

A Boxer's DEFENSE

When fans learned that their boxing hero, Paco Diaz, wrote poetry, they were outraged and demanded that he be banned from the ring. Reporter Dan James spoke to Paco Diaz soon after he was exposed as a poetry lover.

Q: Why don't you tell our readers about what's happened to you, Paco?

P.D: Well, my love of poetry was made public a few months ago, and since that time I've lost most of my fans. I feel so disgruntled, Dan. All I want to do is express myself if I can!

Q: What do you want to say to your fans, Paco?

P.D: My fans have supported me through thick and thin. They stuck by me even when I didn't win. Writing poetry is not a sin. Won't you guys please support me again?

Q: Paco, are you surprised by all the turmoil your poetry writing has caused?

P.D: I am very surprised. There's nothing wrong with poetry in my eyes.

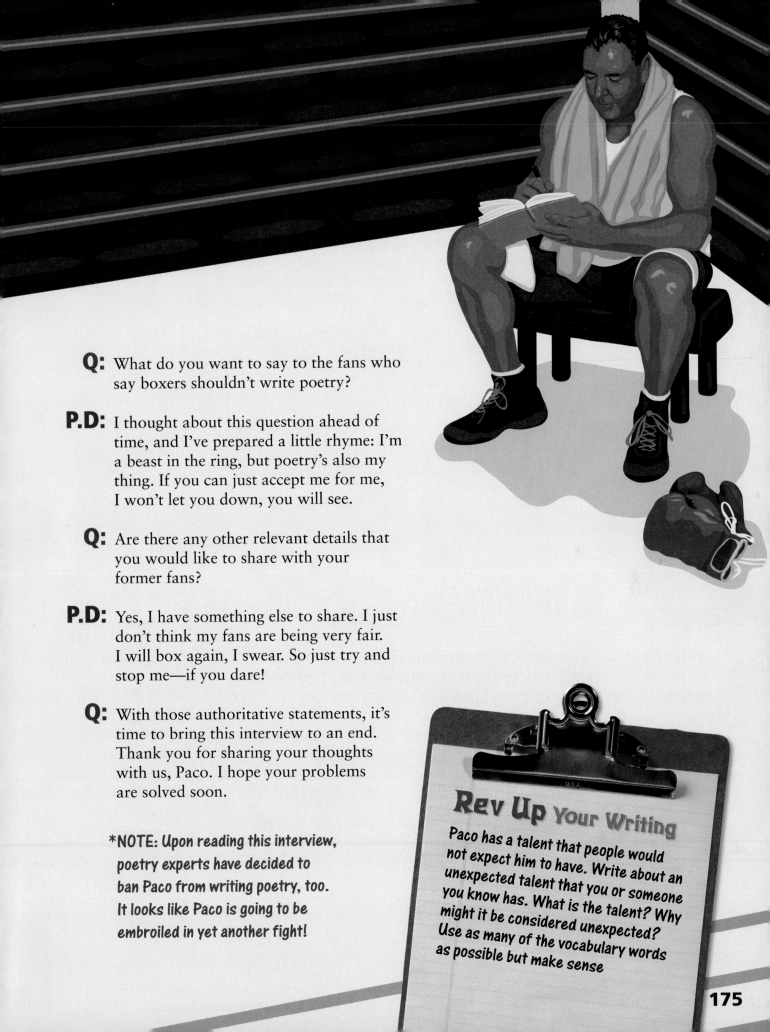

Q: What do you want to say to the fans who say boxers shouldn't write poetry?

P.D: I thought about this question ahead of time, and I've prepared a little rhyme: I'm a beast in the ring, but poetry's also my thing. If you can just accept me for me, I won't let you down, you will see.

Q: Are there any other relevant details that you would like to share with your former fans?

P.D: Yes, I have something else to share. I just don't think my fans are being very fair. I will box again, I swear. So just try and stop me—if you dare!

Q: With those authoritative statements, it's time to bring this interview to an end. Thank you for sharing your thoughts with us, Paco. I hope your problems are solved soon.

*NOTE: Upon reading this interview, poetry experts have decided to ban Paco from writing poetry, too. It looks like Paco is going to be embroiled in yet another fight!

Rev Up Your Writing

Paco has a talent that people would not expect him to have. Write about an unexpected talent that you or someone you know has. What is the talent? Why might it be considered unexpected? Use as many of the vocabulary words as possible but make sense

Can You Relate?

Copy this graphic organizer onto a separate piece of paper. Match the following words with their related vocabulary word. If a word relates to more than one vocabulary word, explain why.

anarchy   Anarchy is a situation in which there are no rules or laws.
commandeer   If you commandeer something, you take it or use it by force.
desultory   If something is desultory, it happens in a random or disorganized way.
ire   If you feel ire, you feel deep anger or fury about something.
provocative   If something is provocative, it is irritating and upsetting.

annex	disgruntled	turmoil

In Your Own Words

Respond to one of the following prompts on a separate piece of paper. As you respond, use as many of the vocabulary words as possible. Be creative but make sense!

▶ Write about a time when hard work paid off for you or someone you know. Explain what happened and describe how it felt to finish.

▶ A fable is a short animal tale that teaches a lesson. Think about an important lesson you've learned during your lifetime. Write a fable that helps teach the lesson to your readers.

▶ Write about a topic of your choice.

VOCABULARY

turmoil
impartiality
authoritative
conclusive
confine
relevant
accommodate
embroil
annex
disgruntled

from The Ordinary Son

By Ron Carlson
Illustrated by Ellen Weinstein

*Would you want to be a genius?
In this short story excerpt, the
narrator uses humor and
wisdom to reflect on what
it means to fill the role
of genius in a family
that is anything but
ordinary.*

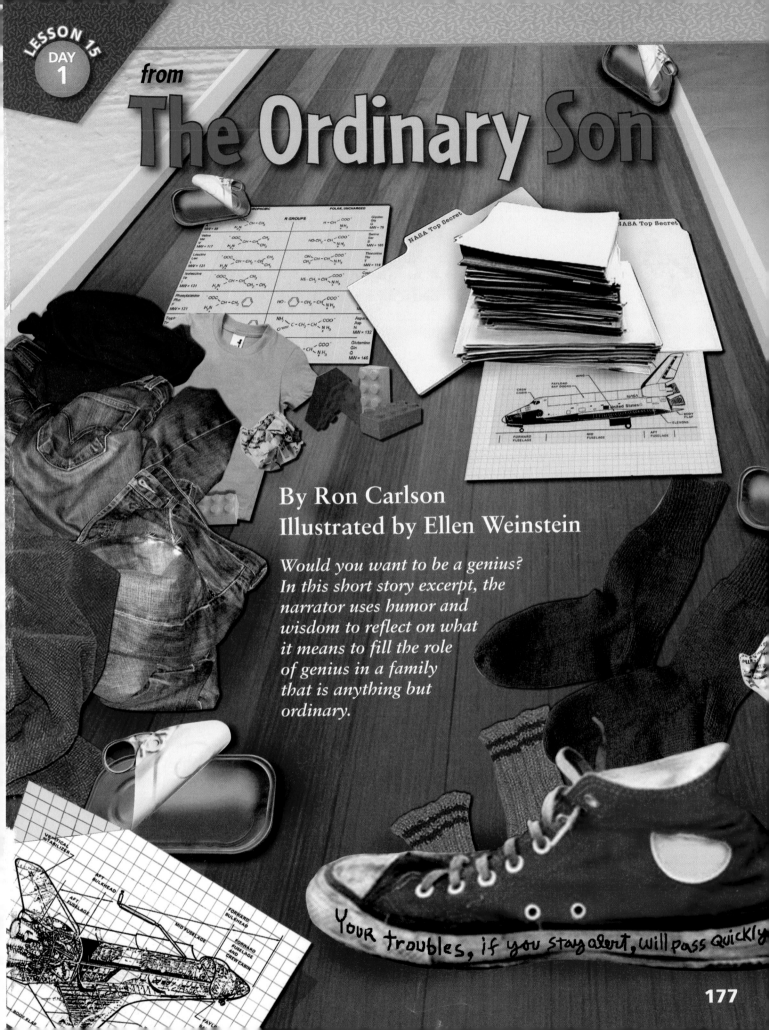

Your troubles, if you stay alert, will pass quickly

Garrett and I took everything in stride.[1] We accepted that ours was a family of geniuses and that we had no telephone or refrigerator or proper beds. We thought it was natural to eat crackers and sardines for months on end. We thought the front yard was supposed to be a jungle of overgrown grass, weeds, and whatever reptiles would volunteer to live there. Twice a year the City of Houston street crew came by and mowed it all down, and daylight would pour in for a month or two. We had no cars. My father was always climbing into white Chevrolet station wagons, unmarked, and going off to the Space Center south of town. My mother was always stepping up into orange VW buses driven by other people and driving off to tour. My sister had been the youngest student at MIT.[2] My brother and I did our own laundry for years and walked to school, where, about seventh grade, we began to see the differences between the way ordinary people lived and the way geniuses lived. Other people's lives, we learned, centered fundamentally on two things: television and soft foods rich with all versions of sugar.

By the time I entered junior high school, my mother's travels had kicked into high gear,[3] so she hired a woman we came to know well, Clovis Armandy, to live with us and to assist in our corporeal[4] care. Gloria Rainstrap's parental theory and practice could be summed up by the verse I heard her recite a thousand times before I reached the age of six: "Feed the soul, the body finds a way." And she fed our souls with a groaning banquet of iron ethics at every opportunity. She wasn't interested in sandwiches or casseroles. She was the kind of person who had a moral motive for her every move. We had no refrigerator because it was simply the wrong way to prolong the value of food, which had little value in the first place. We had no real furniture because furniture became the numbing insulation of drones who worked for the economy, an evil in itself. If religion was the opiate of the masses, then home furnishings were the Novocain[5] of the middle class. Any small surfeit[6] of comfort undermined our moral fabric. We live for the work we can do, not for things, she told us. I've met and heard lots of folks who share Gloria's posture toward life on this earth, but I've never found anyone who could put it so well, present her ideas so convincingly, so beautifully, or so insistently. Her words seduced you into wanting to go without.

FOOTNOTES
....

[1] *took everything in stride:* accepted things without complaint

[2] *MIT:* Massachusetts Institute of Technology

[3] *kicked into high gear:* become very frequent

[4] *corporeal:* physical

[5] *opiate...Novocain:* medicine used to soothe pain

[6] *surfeit:* excess

I won't put any of her poems in this story, but they were transcendent.[7] The Times called her "Buddha's angry daughter." My mother's response to people who were somewhat shocked at our empty house and its unkempt quality was, "We're ego-distant. These little things," she'd say, waving her hand over the litter of the laundry, discarded draft paper, piles of top-secret documents in the hallway, various toys, the odd empty tin of sardines, "don't bother us in the least. We aren't even here for them." I loved that last part and still use it when a nuisance arises: I'm not even here for it. "Ego-distant," my friend Jeff Schreckenbah used to say, standing in our empty house, "which means your ma doesn't sweat the small stuff."

My mother's quirk, one she fostered, was writing on the bottom of things. She started it because she was always gone, for months at a time, and she wanted us to get her messages throughout her absence and thereby be reminded of making correct decisions and ethical choices. It was not unusual to find ballpoint-pen lettering on the bottoms of our shoes and little marker messages on the bottoms of plates, where she'd written in a tiny script. Anything that you could lift up and look under, she would have left her mark on it. These notes primarily confused me. There I'd be in math class and would cross my legs and see something on the edge of my sneaker, and read, "Your troubles, if you stay alert, will pass very quickly away."

I'm not complaining. I never, except once or twice, felt deprived. I like sardines, still. It was a bit of a pinch[8] when I got to high school and noted with new poignancy[9] that I didn't quite have the wardrobe it took to keep up. Geniuses dress plain and clean but not always as clean as their ordinary counterparts, who have nothing better to do with their lives than buy and sort and wash clothes.

Things were fine. I turned seventeen. I was hanging out sitting around my bare room, reading books—the history of this, the history of that, dry stuff—waiting for my genius to kick in. This is what had happened to Christina. One day when she was ten, she was having a tea party with her dolls, which were two rolled pink towels. The next day she'd catalogued and diagrammed the amino acids, laying the groundwork for two artificial sweeteners and a mood elevator.

FOOTNOTES

[7] *transcendent:* beyond the ordinary

[8] *pinch:* difficult situation

[9] *poignancy:* sad feelings

By the time my mother, Gloria Rainstrap, returned from the Northwest, and my father looked up from his table, the State Department "mentors" had been by, and my sister, Christina, was on her way to the inner sanctums of the Massachusetts Institute of Technology. I remember my mother standing against my father's drafting table, her hands along the top. Her jaw was set, and she said, "This is meaningful work for Christina, her special doorway."

My father dragged his eyes up from his drawings, and said, "Where's Christina now?"

So the day I went into Garrett's room and found him writing equations down a huge scroll of butcher paper on which, until that day, he had drawn battle re-creations of the French and Indian Wars, was a big day for me. I stood there in the gloom, watching him crawl along the paper, reeling out figures of which very few were numbers I recognized, most of the symbols being x's and y's and the little twisted members of the Greek alphabet, and I knew that it had skipped me. Genius had cast its powerful, clear eye on me, and said, "No, thanks." At least I was that smart. I realized that I was not going to get to be a genius.

The message took my body a piece at a time, loosening each joint and muscle on the way up and then filling my face with a strange warmth, which I knew immediately was relief.

I was free.

Explain Yourself

Answer each question on a separate piece of paper. Be sure to explain your answers.

1. What are the **fundamentals** of your everyday life? Explain.

2. Would you want to **prolong** a day at school? Why or why not?

3. When might you be **unkempt**? Why?

4. Would you want to **foster** hatred for your worst enemy? Why or why not?

5. What would you feel **deprived** of if you had to attend school on Saturday? Explain.

6. Why would someone spend time in a **sanctum**?

7. Would you **condone** a bully's behavior? Why or why not?

8. What kind of **idiosyncrasy** would you not want to have? Explain.

9. Is being able to express yourself **innate**? Why or why not?

10. How might someone's **paradigm** be affected by bad news?

VOCABULARY

fundamental   The fundamentals of something are its most basic and important parts.

prolong   If you prolong something, you make it last longer.

unkempt   When someone or something is unkempt, it is messy or tangled.

foster   When you foster something, you work to help it grow or continue.

deprive   If you are deprived of something, you are not able to have it.

sanctum   A sanctum is a place that is quiet and private.

condone   If you condone a behavior, you let it happen or accept it.

idiosyncrasy   An idiosyncrasy is a unique or unusual habit.

innate   Something that is innate is an ability or quality that you were born with.

paradigm   Someone's paradigm is the way he or she looks at things or sees the world.

Take It Further

Complete these sentences on a separate piece of paper.

1. Ben was such a **fundamental** part of his baseball team that . . .

2. In order to **prolong** her visit, Tonya decided to . . .

3. Wilson's appearance was **unkempt** after . . .

4. Nika hoped to **foster** the plant's growth by . . .

5. It was obvious that Ruben had been **deprived** of sleep because . . .

6. I consider my bedroom a **sanctum** because . . .

7. Yasmeen's parents would never **condone** . . .

8. Yuri's teacher has an **idiosyncrasy** in which . . .

9. Lauren knew that her singing ability was **innate** because . . .

10. Mr. Richter's **paradigm** helps me understand that . . .

Explore It

Paradigm has a unique spelling and pronunciation—a silent *g!* It's not the only word that has this unique trait, however. Can you think of any others?

Working with others, use the Internet to research other words or use the dictionary to search for words that begin with *gn*. Then write a brief story using as many of the silent *g* words as possible. Be ready to present your findings to the class and make sure you know how to pronounce the words correctly as you share your story!

Superstitious STEVE

SOUTH

"If you swallow gum, it will take seven years to digest. Carrying an acorn around with you will prolong your life."

Growing up, Steve enjoyed learning about superstitions, but his paradigms often got him into a bit of trouble with his friends.

Steve was always terrified of lying for fear that his nose would grow, but sometimes his tongue got the best of him. Afterwards, he stood for hours pressing his nose against the bedroom wall.

One night, he forgot that eating cheese before bed causes nightmares. By his third slice of pizza, he was terrified. He talked to himself all night long and didn't sleep a wink.

Steve started to question his beliefs in his first year in college. His friends didn't care about his unkempt room, but the silly acorn necklace that he promised he would never take off was another thing. His bed that just had to face south towards the bathroom was another. "Facing north will bring me bad health!" he exclaimed. "Dude, you're crazy!" his friends said.

By the time Steve graduated, all his friends thought he was out of his mind.

Maybe my friends are right, he thought. *Maybe I am crazy.*

Then he sat down to polish and eat his daily apple. He had to keep the doctor away, after all.

Crazy SUPERSTITIONS

Don't cross your eyes, they'll get stuck that way!
I would always hear my momma say.
Turns out this rule ain't even the case.
Just a fib to keep you from making a face!

Arthritis is caused by cracking your knuckles.
If you ever hear this, go on and chuckle.
It's a tale mom fostered over the years.
So go crack away, no need to fear!

[Chorus] Tales, tales, crazy tales!
Do you believe these crazy tales?

Don't swim for an hour after having a meal.
If you believe this rule, please get real.
Don't deprive your body before you swim.
You can eat what you want and jump right in.

You shouldn't go outside with wet hair.
You'll catch a cold from the air.
But it's viruses that make you sick.
These superstitions do not stick.

[Chorus] Tales, tales, crazy tales!
Do you believe these
crazy tales?

[Repeat Chorus to Fade]

Rev Up Your Writing

You've just read about superstitions.
What is your opinion of superstitions?
Write a letter to someone that
expresses your opinion. Use as many
of the vocabulary words as possible but
make sense.

Word Organizer

Copy this graphic organizer onto a separate piece of paper.

List things that are fundamental inside a school building and write your answers under the school column. Then list things that are fundamental at a library and write your answers under the library column. Explain your answers.

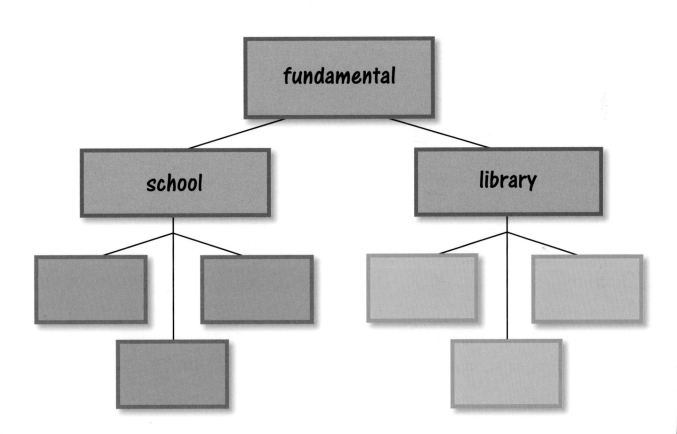

Bon Appétit!

Would you condone dining on a bird's nest? Do you have an appetite for snakes? While these foods may sound unusual to you, people around the world enjoy these and other tasty treats every day. Here is a look at some eating idiosyncrasies from around the world.

MENU

Bird's Nest Soup (Thailand)

The swiftlet, a bird found in Southeast Asia, makes nests out of its own spit. Bird's nest soup made from these nests is such a treat that just one pound can cost almost $1,000! Because of this, nest collectors are willing to climb hundreds of feet to reach the swiftlet's sanctum.

Rattlesnake Salad (United States)

This is quite a common dish! You can have the snake deep-fried, barbecued, or baked, whichever way you prefer it. There seems to be a lot of people with an innate taste for rattlesnake.

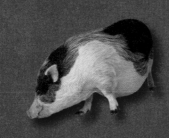

Salo (Ukraine)

Have you ever had pork chops? How about pork fat? Some Ukrainians eat salo, or salted pig fat. In one restaurant, they even serve the pig fat covered in chocolate. What a sweet surprise for unsuspecting tourists!

Who Wants Seconds?

When you sit down for a meal or a snack, you probably don't think about where your food comes from. You might be surprised (and a little grossed out!) to discover the source.

Gelatin   A fundamental part of this wiggly treat used to be made from boiled animal parts—such as hooves, bones, and skin. Yuck!

Honey   This sweet food is actually bee vomit! Bees make honey by drinking nectar and throwing up into a honeycomb.

Cheese   Did you know that bacteria are what make your feet smell? They also give cheese its special odor. Cheese is what is left over when bacteria are added to milk.

Ice Cream   Many types of store-bought ice cream are thickened with part of the kelp plant—a type of slimy seaweed!

Rev Up Your Writing

You've just read about several unusual foods. Write a review of an unusual food that you've tried. Did you enjoy it? Was it what you expected? Would you recommend it? Use as many of the vocabulary words as possible but make sense.

Can You Relate?

Copy this graphic organizer onto a separate piece of paper. Match the following words with their related vocabulary word. If a word relates to more than one vocabulary word, explain why.

endorse When you endorse something, you give support to it.

goad When you goad someone or something, you encourage it to take action.

resign If you resign yourself to something unpleasant, you accept it because you cannot change it.

sanction When you sanction something, you give approval to it.

sustenance Sustenance is food or drink that supports living things.

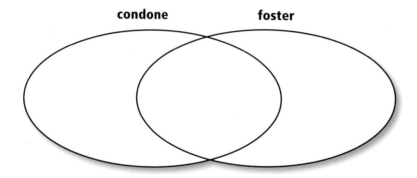

condone   foster

In Your Own Words

Respond to one of the following prompts on a separate piece of paper. As you respond, use as many of the vocabulary words as possible. Be creative but make sense!

► Write about a time when you or someone you know visited a strange place. What was unusual about it? Would you want to return to the place? Why or why not?

► Think of a food that you enjoy or would like to try. Then write a "how to" recipe and explain how to make it step by step.

► Write about a topic of your choice.

VOCABULARY

fundamental
prolong
unkempt
foster
deprive
sanctum
condone
idiosyncrasy
innate
paradigm

based on

The Open Window

By Saki
Illustrated by Sandra Speidel

Following his doctor's orders, Mr. Nuttel seeks rest in the countryside, but while there he hears a story and has an encounter that makes him run for his life.

"My aunt will be down soon, Mr. Nuttel," said a very self-possessed[1] young lady of fifteen. "In the meantime you must try and put up with me."

Framton Nuttel endeavored to flatter the niece. Privately he doubted more than ever whether these formal visits would do much to cure his nervousness.

"I know how it will be," his sister had said when he was preparing to move to the countryside. "You will bury yourself down there[2] and not speak to a living soul, and your nerves will be worse than ever from moping. I shall just give you letters of introduction to all the people I know there. Some of them, as far as I can remember, were quite nice."

Framton wondered whether Mrs. Sappleton, the lady to whom he was presenting one of the letters of introduction, was one of the nice ones.

"Do you know many of the people around here?" asked the niece.

"Hardly a soul," said Framton. "My sister was staying here, at the rectory,[3] you know, some four years ago, and she gave me letters of introduction to some of the people here."

"Then you know practically nothing about my aunt?" pursued the self-possessed young lady.

"Only her name and address," admitted Framton. He was wondering whether Mrs. Sappleton was married or widowed. Something about the room seemed to suggest masculine habitation.

"Her great tragedy," said the girl, "happened just three years ago. That would be since your sister's time."

"Her tragedy?" asked Framton. Somehow, in this restful country spot, tragedies seemed out of place.

"You may wonder," said the niece, "why we keep that window wide open on an October afternoon." She indicated a large French window[4] that opened onto a lawn.

"It is quite warm for the time of the year," said Framton, "but has that window got anything to do with the tragedy?"

"Out through that window, three years ago today, my aunt's husband and her two young brothers went off to hunt birds. They never came back. In crossing the moor,[5] they were all three engulfed in a marsh.[6] It had been that dreadful wet summer, you know, and places that were safe in other years gave way[7] suddenly without warning. Their bodies were never recovered.

FOOTNOTES

[1] *self-possessed:* confident
[2] *bury yourself down there:* stay all alone
[3] *rectory:* the home of a local priest
[4] *French window:* glass doors that open onto a garden or balcony
[5] *moor:* land covered in grasses
[6] *marsh:* swampland
[7] *gave way:* collapsed

That was the dreadful part of it." Here the girl's voice faltered and lost its self-possessed note. "Poor aunt always thinks that they will come back someday, they and the little brown spaniel that was lost with them, and walk in at that window just as they used to do. That is why the window is kept open every evening till it is quite dusk. Poor dear aunt, she has often told me how they went out, her husband with his white waterproof coat over his arm, and Ronnie, her youngest brother, singing, 'Bertie, why do you bound?' as he always did to tease her, because she said it got on her nerves. Do you know, sometimes on still, quiet evenings like this, I almost get a creepy feeling that they will all walk in through that window—"

She broke off[8] with a little shudder. It was a relief to Framton when the aunt bustled into the room with a whirl of apologies for being late.

"I hope Vera has been amusing you," she said.

"She has been very interesting," said Framton.

"I hope you don't mind the open window," said Mrs. Sappleton briskly. "My husband and brothers will be home soon, and they always come in this way. They've been out for snipe[9] in the marshes today, so they'll make a fine mess over my poor carpets."

She rattled on[10] cheerfully about the scarcity of birds and the prospects for duck in the winter. To Framton, it was all purely horrible. He made a desperate effort to turn the talk onto a less ghastly topic. He was conscious that his hostess was giving him only a fragment of her attention. Her eyes were constantly straying past him to the open window and the lawn beyond. It was certainly an unfortunate coincidence that he should have paid his visit on this tragic anniversary.

"The doctors agree in ordering me complete rest, an absence of mental excitement, and an avoidance of physical exercise," announced Framton, who labored under the delusion that total strangers are interested in every detail of one's ailments and infirmities, and their causes and cures.

After discounting Mr. Nuttel with a yawn, Mrs. Sappleton suddenly brightened into alert attention—but not to what Framton was saying.

"Here they are at last!" she cried. "Just in time for tea, and don't they look as if they were muddy up to the eyes!"

Framton shivered slightly and turned toward the niece with a look intended to express sympathetic comprehension. The child was staring out through the open window with dazed horror in her eyes.

FOOTNOTES
8 *broke off:* stopped talking
9 *snipe:* a kind of bird
10 *rattled on:* talked continuously

In a chill shock of nameless fear, Framton swung round in his seat and looked in the same direction.

In the deepening twilight, three figures were walking across the lawn toward the window; one of them was burdened with a white coat hung over his shoulders. A tired brown spaniel kept close at their heels. Noiselessly they neared the house, and then a hoarse young voice chanted out of the dusk: "I said, Bertie, why do you bound?"

Framton grabbed wildly at his stick and hat, swung open the hall door, tore through the gravel drive, and retreated out the front gate. A cyclist coming along the road had to run into the hedge to avoid imminent collision.

"Here we are, my dear," said the bearer of the white coat, coming in through the window. "Fairly muddy, but most of it's dry. Who was that who bolted out as we came up?"

"A most extraordinary man, a Mr. Nuttel," said Mrs. Sappleton. "He could only talk about his illnesses and then dashed off without a word of goodbye or apology when you arrived. One would think he had seen a ghost."

"I expect it was the spaniel," said the niece calmly. "He told me he had a horror of dogs. He was once hunted into a cemetery somewhere on the banks of the Ganges[11] by a pack of wild dogs and had to spend the night in a newly dug grave with the creatures snarling and grinning and foaming just above him. Enough to make anyone lose their nerve."

Making up wild stories at short notice was her specialty.

FOOTNOTES

[11] *Ganges:* a major river in India

Explain Yourself

VOCABULARY

Answer each question on a separate piece of paper. Be sure to explain your answers.

1. If you wanted to qualify for the X Games, in which two sports might you **endeavor** to compete? Why?

2. What might cause you to **falter** when you speak? Explain.

3. What might happen if you drive too **briskly**? Why?

4. Would you like to live in a city with a **scarcity** of rain? Why or why not?

5. If your friend said that he never met a girl who didn't like him, would you call him **delusional**? Why or why not?

6. What kind of **infirmity** might keep you from a great concert? Explain.

7. What might make you **discount** your friend's advice? Explain.

8. How might you be able to tell that a homework assignment is **imminent**?

9. What might give you a clue that a person is being **devious**? Explain.

10. Name a character from a TV show or movie who was **traumatized**. Explain what caused the trauma.

endeavor   When you endeavor to do something, you try your best to do it.

falter   If something falters, it becomes unsteady and may even stop.

briskly   If something is done briskly, it is done quickly and energetically.

scarcity   If there is a scarcity of something, it is difficult to find because there is a very small amount of it.

delusion   A delusion is something that you believe is true but is actually not true.

infirmity   If you have an infirmity, you are weak or sick.

discount   If you discount something, you behave as if it is not important.

imminent   If something is imminent, it is about to happen.

devious   If you are devious, you are dishonest or sneaky.

traumatized   A person is traumatized if something very upsetting happens and has a lasting effect.

Take It Further

Complete these sentences on a separate piece of paper.

1. It is important to practice if you **endeavor** to . . .

2. While practicing his dance routine, Tony suddenly **faltered** when . . .

3. The principal walked **briskly** toward the crowd of students because . . .

4. There is a **scarcity** of boys at our school because . . .

5. I knew my friend Kim was **delusional** when she told me that . . .

6. Mr. Lin's students knew he had a serious **infirmity** after he . . .

7. Paul knew the teacher was **discounting** his excuses when . . .

8. It seemed **imminent** that my computer would crash when . . .

9. Lindsay's plan was **devious** because . . .

10. Aldo has been **traumatized** ever since he saw . . .

Explore It

Words often have more than one meaning. For example, *discount* can mean "ignore" or "lower price."

discount = ignore
You might discount a store's sale if its items are not important to you. If you discount something that is not important to you, you ignore it.

> Have you ever seen an advertisement that you discounted? Describe the ad. Why did you discount the product? What could the advertisers do to make the product more appealing?

discount = lower price
Stores often discount items to encourage you to purchase them. When stores discount items, they reduce their prices.

> Imagine that a store has just discounted an item that you really want to buy. Write an advertisement for the newly discounted item in a way that will make the product appeal to teens.

Lemonade *Disaster*

I needed to make money, so I devised a plan:
some lemons, sugar, water, and cups, and I'd have a lemonade stand!
We were out of lemons, so I substituted limes.
A scarcity of sugar? Well, brown sugar should be fine.

I added sparkling water, 'cause plain just wouldn't do,
and then I went to make a fortune off my fizzing brew.
I had a sign, "Lemonade for $1!" that no doubt would impress
those passing by. I sat and smiled at my imminent success.

My first customer arrived! Ms. McGreevy from next door.
She paid a dollar, took a sip, and spit it on the floor!
"That stuff is nasty! You shouldn't sell it," she advised.
"Anyone who drinks it will be traumatized!"

I didn't respond—how could I? All I could do was stare.
She left without her dollar, which I think is only fair.
I slowly packed my things up based on her advice.
But how to make that money? A bake sale might be nice . . .

Lemonade for $1

A Folktale

The Sea's Revenge

Kuma lived in a small fishing village on a small island in the middle of a big sea. The people of Kuma's village depended on the sea for their survival, and they believed that they must return one-third of what they caught to the sea as an offering of thanks.

One season the fish were not biting. There was a scarcity of food, and people began to go hungry and suffer through terrible infirmities.

In an attempt to find fish, Kuma decided to go farther out into the sea than he had ever gone before. He caught enough fish that day to feed the entire village! Even though Kuma caught more than enough fish for his village, he had the delusion that if he gave the sea back its usual offering, some villagers might still go hungry, so Kuma did not give the sea its usual share.

That night, after the village celebrated and ate their fill of fish, the sea rose from its bed in a giant wave and swept through the village. It entered every hut and went up every path. There was not one corner of the village untouched by the sea's arm.

When the villagers awoke in the morning, they discovered that the sea had taken all of the remaining fish. It had taken back the offering Kuma should have given it.

Never again did a fisherman ignore the offering of thanks. From that day forth, half of every catch was returned to the sea.

Rev Up Your Writing

Write about a time when something unexpected happened because of a decision you made. What could you have done differently? What did you learn? Use as many of the vocabulary words as possible but make sense.

Word Organizer

Copy this graphic organizer onto a separate piece of paper.

Scarcity is near the cold end of the Word-O-Meter. Think of words that would be hotter or colder. Write your answers in the boxes. Explain your answers.

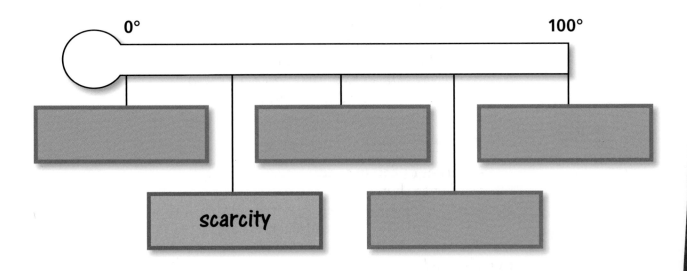

0°　　　　　　　　　　　　　　　　　　　　　　　100°

scarcity

Q: **What's more traumatizing than finding a worm in your apple?**

A: Finding half a worm in your apple!

THE FIREFIGHTERS OF THE 104TH

The firefighters of the 104th
Went out one day heading north.
They never faltered on their way to the fire.
Their sirens and horns rang higher and higher.

They reached a house overcome by flames,
Readied their hoses and took aim.
It was then they heard the fearful cries,
And suddenly they realized

There were people in those burning rooms
Just minutes away from their doom.
Some of the firefighters continued to spray
While the others endeavored to save the day.

Five ran into the smoke and fire
Into the dangerous, burning pyre.
Then one neighbor let out a gasp,
And everyone watched as the roof collapsed.

But as the smoke cloud started to clear,
Those still outside let out a cheer.
Seven figures, not five, were making their way.
The 104th had saved the day.

April FOOL

In my family, April Fool's Day is the most anticipated day of the year. Last year, my sister got me good: she deviously changed the time on my bedside clock. When my alarm went off, I got up and got ready for school before realizing it was only 5 A.M.!

I wanted revenge this year.

Once we got home from soccer practice, my plan was to invite her out for ice cream. When we got there, I'd say that I was going to the restroom, but instead I would sneak out the back door and come home, leaving her there to wait for hours.

When we got home from practice, I started my plan.

"Would you like to get some ice cream with me?" I asked sweetly.

"Sure," she replied. "But we have to go right now. You don't have time to shower."

Since she tricked me every year, I wasn't going to discount anything she said. Her telling me not to shower seemed suspicious. Was she just trying to make me go out into public looking horrible? Was that her April Fool's trick? I wasn't going to let her get me again.

"I'll be really quick!" I promised, running to the bathroom for a brisk shower.

I was proud of myself as I got in and turned on the shower.

All of a sudden, bright orange water rained down all over me! I was so shocked that I couldn't move. Then I noticed a faint orange smell. I licked my arm . . . and tasted orange juice! She had put a powdered drink mix inside the showerhead!

I screamed and struggled to turn off the orange shower. Outside, I could hear my sister laughing.

Looks like she got me again.

Rev Up Your Writing

You've read about two disastrous situations. Write about a disaster you've heard about or have experienced. Use as many of the vocabulary words as possible but make sense.

Can You Relate?

Copy this graphic organizer onto a separate piece of paper. Match the following words with their related vocabulary word. If a word relates to more than one vocabulary word, explain why.

afflict If something afflicts you, it causes you to suffer.
burgeoning If something is burgeoning, it is developing quickly.
lethargic A lethargic person is tired and lacks energy.
ruse A person with a ruse has a plan to deceive others.
vindictive A vindictive person is seeking revenge.

devious	imminent	infirmity

In Your Own Words

Respond to one of the following prompts on a separate piece of paper. As you respond, use as many of the vocabulary words as possible. Be creative but make sense!

▶ Write about a time you or someone you know made up a story. What was the situation? Did anyone believe the story? What happened?

▶ A natural disaster has destroyed your community. Write a letter requesting emergency funds from the federal government. Describe the disaster and its effects. Present a plan for rebuilding.

▶ Write about a topic of your choice.

VOCABULARY

endeavor
falter
briskly
scarcity
delusion
infirmity
discount
imminent
devious
traumatized

Glossary

A

accommodate (uh KOM uh dayt) If you accommodate others, you give them what they need or want.

accustomed (uh KUHS tuhmd) If you are accustomed to something, you are so used to it that it seems normal and comfortable.

adulation (AJ uh LAY shuhn) Adulation is a feeling of deep admiration or worship.

adversity (ad VUR suh tee) Adversity is an extremely difficult experience or situation that is hard to overcome.

advocate (AD vuh kiht) When you are an advocate of something, you publicly support it and believe in it.

affinity (uh FIHN uh tee) If you have an affinity for someone or something, you have a natural attraction to it.

agility (uh JIHL uh tee) Someone with agility moves with speed and skill.

agonize (AG uh nyz) If you agonize about something, you worry about it for a long time.

annex (AN ehks) When a place has been annexed, it has been taken over.

appease (uh PEEZ) When you appease people, you give them what they want to stop them from being angry.

aptitude (AP tuh tood) Aptitude is the natural ability to learn something quickly and do it well.

arbiter (AHR buh tuhr) An arbiter is someone who settles disagreements.

authoritative (uh THAWR uh TAY tihv) An authoritative person is powerful and knowledgeable.

autonomy (aw TAWN uh mee) If you have autonomy, you are independent and free to make your own choices.

B

briskly (brihsk lee) If something is done briskly, it is done quickly and energetically.

bristle (BRIHS uhl) If you bristle toward someone or something, you act in an angry or irritated way toward it.

C

callous (KAL uhs) If something is callous, it is thick skinned or insensitive.

cantankerous (kan TANG kuhr uhs) A cantankerous person complains or argues about everything.

capsize (KAP syz) If a boat is capsized, it is turned over.

cavalier (KAV uh LIHR) A cavalier person doesn't take important situations seriously.

chastise (chas TYZ) When you chastise people, you scold them for their misbehavior.

complacent (kuhm PLAY sehnt) If you are complacent, you don't think that you need to worry or do anything about a situation.

conclusive (kuhn KLOO sihv) If something is conclusive, it is final or certain.

condescending (KON dih SEHND ihng) When you are condescending to others, you talk down to them, making them feel unimportant or stupid.

condone (kuhn DOHN) If you condone a behavior, you let it happen or accept it.

confine (kuhn FYN) A person who is confined to a place is kept from leaving it.

congenial (kuhn JEEN ee yuhl) People who are congenial are friendly and easy to get along with.

contrite (kuhn TRYT) If you are contrite, you are very sorry or ashamed.

D

deftly (dehft lee) Something that is done deftly is done with skill and speed.

deliberate (dih LIHB uhr iht) A deliberate action is one that is done on purpose, often slowly and with care.

delusion (dih LOO zhuhn) A delusion is something that you believe is true but is actually not true.

deprive (dih PRYV) If you are deprived of something, you are not able to have it.

devious (DEE vee uhs) If you are devious, you are dishonest or sneaky.

devour (dih VOWR) If you devour something, you eat it eagerly and quickly.

disconcerting (DIHS kuhn SURT ihng) When something is disconcerting, it is disturbing because it seems odd.

discount (dihs KOWNT) If you discount something, you behave as if it is not important.

discredit (dihs KREHD iht) When you discredit people, you hurt their reputation by pointing out what they have done wrong.

disgruntled (dihs GRUHN tuhld) If you are disgruntled, you are angry and dissatisfied.

disposition (DIHS puh ZIHSH uhn) Your disposition is your personality or mood.

distinct (dihs TIHNGKT) If something is distinct, it is clear or obvious.

divergent (dy VUR juhnt) Things that are divergent become more and more different from each other over time.

dogged (DAWG ihd) Someone who is dogged is determined to do something even if it is very difficult.

dupe (doop) When you dupe others, you fool or trick them.

E

edible (EHD uh buhl) If something is edible, it is safe to eat.

embed (ehm BEHD) If you embed something, you set it deeply inside something else.

embroil (ehm BROYL) If you are embroiled in something, you are mixed up in something bad, such as a fight.

emit (ih MIHT) To send out or give off something is to emit it.

emulate (EHM yuh layt) If you emulate someone, you try to be like that person because you admire him or her.

endeavor (ehn DEHV uhr) When you endeavor to do something, you try your best to do it.

engross (ehn GROHS) If something engrosses you, it takes up your full attention.

enunciate (ih NUHN see ayt) If you enunciate a word, you pronounce it very clearly.

epiphany (ih PIHF uh nee) When you have an epiphany, you suddenly understand something clearly or have a great idea.

equivocate (ih KWIHV uh KAYT) When you equivocate, you avoid telling the truth by not giving a direct answer.

essential (uh SEHN shuhl) Something that is essential is absolutely necessary.

euphoric (yoo FAWR ihk) When you are euphoric, you are extremely happy.

evoke (ih VOHK) If something evokes thoughts or feelings, it brings them to mind.

exasperate (ehg ZAS puh rayt) If someone or something exasperates you, it makes you very angry or frustrated.

exclusion (ehk SKLOO zhuhn) An exclusion is something that has been left out on purpose.

exemplify (ehg ZEHM pluh fy) If you exemplify something, you are an outstanding example of it.

exotic (ehg ZOT ihk) Something that is exotic is unusual and interesting because it comes from a faraway place.

F

falter (FAWL tuhr) If something falters, it becomes unsteady and may even stop.

fanfare (FAN fair) Fanfare is music or a showy display celebrating someone or something important.

fervor (FUR vuhr) If you do something with fervor, you do it with great energy and dedication.

foist (foyst) If you foist something on people, you force it on them.

foster (FAWS tuhr) When you foster something, you work to help it grow or continue.

frenzy (FREHN zee) Someone in a frenzy is so excited or nervous that he or she is nearly out of control.

fundamental (FUHN duh MEHN tuhl) The fundamentals of something are its most basic and important parts.

fusion (FYOO zhuhn) Fusion is when two or more things are combined or fused together so that they can't come apart.

G

galvanize (GAL vuh nyz) If you galvanize a group of people, you motivate or inspire them to act.

graphically (GRAF uh kuhl lee) When people describe something graphically, they use so much detail that you feel like you can see it.

grotesque (groh TEHSK) If you think something looks grotesque, it looks so strange that it disturbs you.

H

haphazard (HAP HAZ uhrd) If something is haphazard, it is unplanned, disorganized, or messy.

hermit (HUR miht) A hermit is someone who lives alone, far away from other people.

hostile (HOS tuhl) Someone who is hostile is angry and may act in a mean or dangerous way.

hypocrisy (hih POK ruh see) Hypocrisy is saying you believe something but acting in a different way.

I

idiosyncrasy (IHD ee uh SIHNG kruh see) An idiosyncrasy is a unique or unusual habit.

imminent (IHM uh nuhnt) If something is imminent, it is about to happen.

impartiality (IHM pahr shee AL uh tee) Someone who acts with impartiality acts fairly and does not favor one side over another.

impressionable (ihm PREHSH uh nuh buhl) If you are impressionable, you are easily influenced by others.

indifferent (ihn DIHF uhr uhnt) If you are indifferent to something, you are not for or against it.

indulgent (ihn DUHL juhnt) If you are indulgent, you enjoy giving others whatever they want.

infirmity (ihn FUR muh tee) If you have an infirmity, you are weak or sick.

infuriate (ihn FYUR ee ayt) When someone or something infuriates you, it makes you extremely angry, even furious.

innate (ih NAYT) Something that is innate is an ability or quality that you were born with.

insinuate (ihn SIHN yu ayt) If you insinuate something, you hint that it is true without actually saying it.

intone (ihn TOHN) If you intone something, you say it slowly and clearly and in a flat, dull voice.

intricate (IHN truh kiht) Something that is intricate is complicated or difficult because it has many details or small parts.

invariably (ihn VAIR ee uh blee) When something happens invariably, it always happens when you expect it to.

invigorating (ihn VIHG uh rayt ihng) Something that is invigorating makes you feel full of new energy.

L

laudable (LAW duh buhl) If something is laudable, it is so good it deserves to be praised or rewarded.

lilting (lihl tihng) If a sound is lilting, it is pleasantly light and musical.

lithe (lyth) A lithe person is flexible and moves gracefully.

livid (LIHV ihd) People who are livid are extremely angry.

M

maniacal (muh NY uh kuhl) When you act maniacal, you act wild and crazy, like a maniac.

memento (muh MEHN toh) A memento is an object that you keep because it reminds you of a special person or occasion.

merciless (MUR sih lihs) When you are merciless, you act cruelly and show no concern, pity, or mercy.

methodical (muh THOD uh kuhl) Someone who is methodical does things very carefully and step by step.

meticulous (muh TIHK yuh luhs) Someone who is meticulous does things very carefully and with great attention to detail.

muted (MYOO tihd) Muted colors and sounds are gentle and soft, not strong and bright.

mutiny (MYOO tuh nee) If you mutiny, you rebel against your leader or whoever is in charge.

N

narcissistic (NAHR sih SIHS tihk) People who are narcissistic think mostly about themselves and admire themselves greatly.

O

omniscient (om NIHSH uhnt) Someone who is omniscient knows or seems to know everything.

oppress (uh PREHS) When you oppress people, you take away their freedom to make their own decisions.

P

painstakingly (PAYNZ TAY kihng lee) When you do something painstakingly, you do it very slowly and carefully.

palatable (PAL uh tuh buhl) Food that is palatable is acceptable to eat but not delicious.

paradigm (PAR uh dihm) Someone's paradigm is the way he or she looks at things or sees the world.

pedestrian (puh DEHS tree uhn) Something that is pedestrian is so common or ordinary that it is not interesting.

pervade (puhr VAYD) If something pervades an area, it spreads throughout.

pessimism (PEHS uh mihz uhm) Pessimism is when you expect the worst or see only the negative side of things.

placate (PLAY kayt) If you placate someone, you make that person less angry by doing something to please him or her.

ponder (PON duhr) If you ponder something, you think about it carefully.

pretense (PREE tehns) A pretense is something you do or say to make people believe something that is not true.

prolong (pruh LONG) If you prolong something, you make it last longer.

pronouncement (pruh NOWNS muhnt) Pronouncements are formal orders or announcements.

protrude (proh TROOD) If something protrudes, it sticks out.

purse (purs) If you purse your lips, you press them together tightly.

Q

quizzical (KWIHZ uh kuhl) If you are quizzical about something, you question it or doubt it.

R

raucous (RAW kuhs) Something that is raucous is loud and rowdy.

ravage (RAV ihj) When something is ravaged, it is so badly damaged that it is destroyed.

recollect (REHK uh LEHKT) If you recollect something, you remember it.

rectitude (REHK tuh tood) A person with rectitude has a strong and honest personality.

refinement (rih FYN muhnt) If you show refinement, you act politely and show good taste.

relevant (REHL uh vuhnt) If something is relevant, it is connected to what is being talked about at the time.

reminisce (REHM uh NIHS) When you reminisce, you think back on good things from the past that you miss.

renowned (rih NOWND) People who are renowned are famous for their skill or talent.

repress (rih PREHS) If you repress a feeling, you hold it back or keep it inside.

repugnant (rih PUHG nuhnt) If something is repugnant to you, you dislike it so much that it disgusts you.

repulse (rih PUHLS) If something repulses you, it disgusts you so much that you want to get away from it.

reverberate (rih VUR buh rayt) If a loud sound reverberates, it echoes around you and seems to shake the place you are in.

reverence (REHV uhr uhns) If you have reverence for someone, you show that person deep respect.

rudimentary (ROO duh MEHN tuhr ee) Something that is rudimentary is very simple and not completely developed.

S

salvage (SAL vihj) If you salvage something, you save it from destruction.

sanctum (SANGK tuhm) A sanctum is a place that is quiet and private.

satirical (suh TIHR uh kuhl) Something that is satirical uses humor to show how foolish or wicked a person or idea is.

scarcity (SKAIR suh tee) If there is a scarcity of something, it is difficult to find because there is a very small amount of it.

secular (SEHK yuh luhr) If something is secular, it has nothing to do with religion.

sentimental (SEHN tuh MEHN tuhl) Someone who is sentimental about things has tender and loving feelings about them.

simulate (SIHM yuh layt) When you simulate something, you pretend that you are doing it.

simultaneously (SY muhl TAY nee uhs lee) When things happen simultaneously, they happen at the same time.

stalwart (STOL wuhrt) If you are stalwart, people can depend on you to be loyal and hard working.

stoic (STOH ihk) A stoic person doesn't show any emotion, even when bad things happen.

subservient (suhb SUR vee uhnt) If you are subservient, you do whatever someone else wants you to do.

surreptitious (SUR uhp TIHSH uhs) Someone who is surreptitious is secretive and sneaky.

swath (swoth) A swath is a long, wide strip or path.

T

tentative (TEHN tuh tihv) If something is tentative, it is planned to happen but not certain.

tinge (tihnj) A tinge is a small amount of something, such as color or feeling.

traumatized (TRAW muh tyzd) A person is traumatized if something very upsetting happens and has a lasting effect.

trudge (truhj) When you trudge, you walk with slow, heavy steps.

turmoil (TUR moyl) Things are in turmoil when they are confused and out of order.

U

unequivocal (UHN ih KWIHV uh kuhl) If something is unequivocal, it cannot be misinterpreted because it is completely clear and obvious.

unkempt (uhn KEHMPT) When someone or something is unkempt, it is messy or tangled.

unsurpassed (UHN suhr PAST) When someone or something is unsurpassed, it is better than everything else.

urgent (UR juhnt) If something is urgent, it needs to be taken care of immediately.

V

vague (vayg) When something is vague, it is so unclear that it is hard to understand.

venerable (VEHN uhr uh buhl) Venerable people deserve respect because they are old and wise.

vigorously (VIHG uhr uhs lee) When you do something vigorously, you do it with lots of energy.

voracious (vuh RAY shuhs) If you have a voracious appetite, you are extremely hungry and can hardly be satisfied.

W

wary (WAIR ee) If you are wary about something, you are worried that it might be dangerous or cause problems.

wile (wyl) Someone or something that wiles others tricks them into doing something.

wiry (WYR ee) Someone who is wiry is thin but strong.

Acknowledgments

Grateful acknowledgment is given to the following sources for illustrations and photography:

Illustration

Pp.8-9, 11 Ron Mahoney; pp.20-21, 23 Fred Willingham; p.32a Durga Bernhard; p.32b Jared Montano; pp.33-34 Durga Bernhard; p.35 Jared Montano; p.41 Judy DuFour Love; pp.44-45, 47 Lin Wang; p.53 Joe Bucco; pp.63-64 Shayne Letain; p.66 Aaron Jasinski; p.75 Drew Rose; p.77 Octavio Diaz; p.80 Denny Bond; pp.92-93, 96 Judith Hunt; p.99 Carlos Castellanos; p.115 Nancy Harrison; pp.128-129, 131 Jared Osterhold; p.150 Bob Doucet; p.159 Bill Petersen; pp.164-165, 168 Micha Archer; p.174 Chris Lyons; pp.177-178, 180 Ellen Weinstein; p.183 Wendy Rasmussen; pp.189-190, 192 Sandra Speidel; p.195 Brandon Reese; p.196 Paula Wendland; p.199 Qi Wang.

Photography

P.14a ©Brand X Pictures/Getty Images; p.14b Public Domain; pp.14–15 ©PhotoDisc/Getty Images; p.15a ©Corbis; p.15b ©The Stapleton Collection/Bridgeman Art Library (New York); p.15c ©Artville/Getty Images; p.17a ©Bob Elsdale/The Image Bank Getty Images; p.17b ©Mary Evans Picture Library/Everett Collection, Inc.; p.18a ©Dwayne Brown/Brownstock/Alamy Images; p.18b ©StockTrek/Getty Images; p.18c ©Artville/Getty Images; p.26a ©Stringer/Getty Images; p.26b ©GK Hart/Vikki Hart/The Image Bank/Getty Images; pp.26–27 ©PhotoDisc/Getty Images; p.27a ©Getty Images; p.27b ©PhotoDisc/Getty Images; p.27c ©Artville/Getty Images; p.29 ©Camera Press/Redux Pictures; p.30a © Atlantide Phototravel/Corbis; p.30b ©Ocean/Corbis; p.30c ©Artville/Getty Images; pp.38–39a ©John Coletti/Photodisc/Getty Images; pp.38–39b ©Bettmann/Corbis; p.39a ©Philip Game/Alamy; p.39b ©Visions of America/Superstock; p.39c ©Artville/Getty Images; p.42 ©Artville/Getty Images; p.50 ©Hulton-Deutsch Collection/Corbis; p.51a ©The Granger Collection, New York — All rights reserved; p.51b Comstock Images/Getty Images; p.51c Courtesy of Harold G. Craighead, School of Applied and Engineering Physics, Cornell University; p.51d ©Artville/Getty Images; p.53a ©Givaga/Alamy Images; p.53b HA Collection/Ingram Publishing Limited; p.54a ©PunchStock; p.54b ©Getty Images; p.54c ©Artville/Getty Images; p.56 ©Michael O'Niel/Corbis Outline; p.57 ©Ed Freeman/Taxi/Getty Images; p.60 ©Rainer Hackenberg/zefa/Corbis; p.63 ©Corbis; pp.64, 67 ©Artville/Getty Images; pp.69–70 ©Library of Congress Prints & Photographs Division; p.71 ©Hulton Archive/Getty Images; p.75 ©Artville/Getty Images; p.78a ©Corbis; p.78b ©Kate Powers/Getty Images; p.81 ©Getty Images; p.83 ©Bob Peterson/Getty Images; p.86a ©David LeFranc/Corbis KIPA; p.86b ©Steve Pope/epa/Corbis; p.86c ©Kevin Sullivan/Orange County Register/Corbis; p.87a ©Fernando Leon/Stringer/Getty Images; p.87b © Artville/Getty Images; p.89 ©Vishnukumar Sivaraman/Age Fotostock America, Inc.; p.90a ©Kuzma/Alamy Images; p.90b ©Artville/Getty Images; p.99 ©PhotoSlinger/Alamy Images; p.100a ©Getty Images; p.100b ©PhotoDisc/Getty Images; p.100c ©PhotoDisc/Getty Images; p.100d ©Corbis; p.100e ©Artville/Getty Images; p.101 ©PhotoDisc/Getty Images; p.102a, c ©Redmond Durrell/Alamy Images; pp.102–103 ©Getty Images; p.103a ©David J. Green/Alamy; p.103 ©Comstock Images/Getty Images; p.103 ©Ocean/Corbis; p.103 ©PhotoDisc/Getty Images; p.103 ©G. K. & Vikki Hart/PhotoDisc/Getty Images; p.103 ©Artville/Getty Images; p.105a ©Radius Images/Alamy; p.105b ©James Woodson/Getty Images; p.106 ©Houghton Mifflin Harcourt; p.108 ©RadiusImages/Alamy; p.111a ©Yury Shirokov/Alamy Images; p.111b ©Ciaran Griffin/Stockbyte/Getty Images; p.111c, d ©George Doyle/Stockbyte/Getty Images; p.112a ©Yury Shirokov/Alamy Images; p.112b ©Angelo Cavalli/Photodisc/Getty Images; p.112c ©Erik Isakson/Rubberball Productions/Getty Images; p.112d ©Artville/Getty Images; p.114a ©BBC/Corbis; p.114b ©Lynn Goldsmith/Corbis; p.114c ©Brian Bahr/AFP/Getty Images; p.115a ©LGI Stock/Corbis; p.115b ©Bettmann/Corbis; p115c ©Artville/Getty Images; p.117 ©Andrew D. Berstein/NBAE/Getty Images; p.118 ©Photodisc/Getty Images; p.119 ©Focus on Sport/Getty Images; p.122a ©Bill Hatcher/National Geographic/Getty Images; p.122b ©Tom Bol/Tom Bol Photo; p.123a ©Getty Images; p.123b ©Artville/Getty Images; p.125a ©Zoonar/Martina I Me/Age Fotostock America, Inc.; p.125b ©Getty Images; p.125c ©Comstock Images/Getty Images; p.126a ©Getty Images; p.126b ©Atlantide Phototravel/Corbis; p.126c ©Frans Lemmens/The Image Bank/Getty Images; p. 126d ©Artville/Getty Images; p.134a ©PhotoDisc/Getty Images; p.134b ©Europics/NewsCom; p.134c ©PhotoSpin, Inc./Alamy Images; pp.134–135 ©Matthew Kulka/zefa/Corbis; p.135a ©Peter Cade/Getty Images; p.135b ©Artville/Getty Images; p.137a ©Judith Collins/Alamy; p.137b ©Judith Collins/Alamy; p.137c ©Index Stock Imagery, Inc/Photolibrary; p.137d ©Estate Of Keith Morris/Redferns/Getty Images; p.138a ©Hypermania Stock Photography/ Alamy; p.138b ©PhotoDisc/Getty Images; p.138c ©C Squared Studios/Photodisc/Getty Images; ©Artville/Getty Images; p.140 ©Richard Nowitz/Getty Images; pp.141–142 ©Ingram Publishing/SuperStock; pp.143–144 ©Food Collection/SuperStock; p.148 ©Artville/Getty Images; pp.150–151 ©Michael Beiriger/Alamy; p.151a ©Photodisc/Getty Images; p.151b ©Magnus Johansson/Cutcaster; p.151c ©The Food Passionates/Corbis; p.151d ©Artville/Getty Images; p.153 ©Ken Fisher/Stone/Getty Images; p.154 ©Digital Studios; p.154 ©Tim Fuller; p.155 ©Deborah Feingold/Corbis; p.158a ©Getty Images; p.158b ©Kent Knudson/Getty Images; p.158c ©Yongyut Khasawaong/Alamy Images; p.159 ©Artville/Getty Images; p.161a ©John Foxx/Getty Images; p.161b ©Kelly Harriger/Corbis; p.161c ©Sam Dudgeon/Houghton Mifflin Harcourt; p.161d ©Robert Essel NYC/Corbis; p.161e ©AbleStock/Index Stock Imagery/Photolibrary; p.162a ©Charlie Drevstam/Getty Images; p.162b ©John A Rizzo/Getty Images; p.162c ©Artville/Getty Images; p.171a ©Getty Image; p.171b ©Bettmann/Corbis; p.171c ©Comstock Images/Getty Images; p.171d ©Lew Robertson/Corbis; p.172a ©Stock Montage/SuperStock; p.172b, c ©Comstock Images/Getty Images; p.172d ©Artville/Getty Images; p.174 ©Getty Images; p.175 ©Artville/Getty Images; p.184a ©BananaStock/JupiterImages/Getty Images; p.184b ©Artville/Getty Images; p.186a ©AndyLim.com/Alamy; p.186b ©Comstock Images/Getty Images; p.186c, d ©Getty Images; pp.186–187a ©Pestrikov/Fotolia; pp.186–187 b,c ©Getty Images; p.187a ©Andrew Unangst/Alamy Images; p.187b ©Getty Images; p.187c ©Image Source/Punchstock; p.195 ©Comstock Images/Getty Images; p.196 ©Artville/Getty Images; p.197 ©Lushpix/Fotosearch; p.198 ©Chris Cheadle/Getty Images; p.199 ©Artville/Getty Images.